NEWTON PAGE

NEWTON PAGE

NICHOLAS BARBON

THE COMPLETE WORKS:

ECONOMICS, TRADE, BUILDING AND INSURANCE

By

Nicholas Barbon

Edited by

Gavin John Adams

NEWTON PAGE

NEWTON PAGE

www.newtonpage.com

Nicholas Barbon
The Complete Works:
Economics, Trade, Building and Insurance

By
Nicholas Barbon
Edited by
Gavin John Adams

A Discourse Shewing the Great Advantages that New-buildings and the Enlarging of Towns and Cities do Bring to a Nation (1678); A Letter to a Gentleman in the Country, Giving an Account of the Two Insurance - Offices; the Fire-Office & Friendly-Society (1684); An Apology for the Builder: or a Discourse Shewing the Cause and Effects of the Increase of Building (1685); A Discourse of Trade (1690); An Answer to Paper Entituled,Reasons against Reducing Interest to Four per Cent. (1694); A Discourse Concerning Coining the New Money lighter. In Answer to Mr. Lock's Considerations about raising the Value of Money (1696).

Published by Newton Page 2019

1 3 5 7 9 10 8 6 4 2

ISBN 978-1-934619-18-6
Library of Congress Control Number: 2019935036

Printed in the United States of America
Set in Adobe Garamond Pro

CONTENTS

NOTE ON THE TEXT

Since each of the books and pamphlets contained in this collection were first published in the late seventeenth-century, conventions of spelling, grammar, punctuation, expression, vocabulary and general notation have each undergone considerable modernization. In addition, the relatively crude practices of seventeenth-century book and pamphlet production have been gradually replaced by the radically more exacting standards of modern publishing, which demand both uniformity of typesetting and editorial consistency. As a consequence of those changes, the modern reader is used to a more polished product than those available in the past.

However, notwithstanding the usual expectations of the modern reader, and in full appreciation that the original texts are not as easy on the modern eye as they would have been on their contemporary equivalents, the temptation to edit them to conform with modern writing and publishing conventions has been resisted. That approach has been taken because to do anything other than retain the original form of the texts would be to detract from their colorful character. The only two minor exceptions to that approach have been the correction of dischordant italics and the replacement of the medial s with the modern s.

Each of the books were written for the consideration of

the inhabitants of Great Britain. As such, each is tailored to conform with the conventional seventeenth-century stylistic expectations of a British readership. American readers will notice that in maintaining the integrity of the original publications, the original historic British forms of spelling have been retained. More generally, readers will notice both inconsistent and imaginative forms of spelling throughout.

Reproduced in this collection are the first editions and printings of:

A Discourse Shewing the Great Advantages that New-buildings and the Enlarging of Towns and Cities do Bring to a Nation. London (1678)

A Letter to a Gentleman in the Country, Giving an Account of the Two Insurance - Offices; the Fire-Office & Friendly-Society. (1684)

An Apology for the Builder: or a Discourse Shewing the Cause and Effects of the Increase of Building. London: Printed for Cave Pullen at the Angel in St. Pauls-Church-yard (1685)

A Discourse of Trade. London: Printed by Tho. Milbourn for the Author (1690)

An Answer to Paper Entituled,Reasons against Reducing Interest to Four per Cent. (1694)

A Discourse Concerning Coining the New Money lighter. In Answer to Mr. Lock's Considerations about raising the Value of Money. London: Printed for Richard Chiswell, at the Rose and Crown in St. Paul's Church-Yard. (1696)

A

DISCOURSE

SHEWING THE

GREAT ADVANTAGES

THAT

New-Buildings,

And the Enlarging of

Towns and Cities

Do bring to a NATION.

LONDON,

Printed *Anno Domini*, 1678.

A

DISCOURSE

SHEWING THE GREAT ADVANTAGES

THAT NEW-BUILDINGS

AND THE ENLARGING OF TOWNS AND CITIES

DO BRING TO A NATION

LONDON,

PRINTED ANNO DOMINI, 1678

(1678)

A DISCOURSE SHEWING THE GREAT ADVANTAGES THAT NEW-BUILDINGS AND THE ENLARGING OF TOWNS AND CITIES DO BRING TO A NATION.

There is nothing that is more the interest of the Prince, or Governours; or which conduceth more to the present Prosperity, or future greatness of a Nation, then to incourage the Builders of Houses; And yet by a general mistake, nothing of late hath been though more prejudicial and destructive to it; The reason of this great mistake, seems to arise from those two Calamities that fell on this Nation one year after another (viz.) the Plague, and Fire of London; For by the first, 200000 people dying in one year, the fall of Rents of the Land was occasioned; Corn, Meat, and Wooll, that was wont to Feed and Cloath these 200000 persons, now wanting Vent, occasioned the Market to fall, for the price of the Land must follow the Price of its Comodities: By the latter, thouhg not an immediate cause; yet the City being re built faster then the Inhabitants could remove, by reason of Leases and other circum stances that detained them, the fall and loss of Rent in the Houses was occasioned; and thus the Country and City being both loserss do (as losers often use to do) lay the fault on their best Friends, and charge there want of Tennants to their Land and Houses on the increase of the New-Buildings in the Suburbs. The first saying, that it drew the People out of the Countrey, and so Depopulated the Conntrey; And the latter, that it ruined the City by taking away the Trade of it.

But how great this mistake is, and how unjust these accusations are, will appear by the following discourse.

There are two things that are the common interest of all Princes and Governours in the world, where there is property of Land.

First, to preserve and increase the number of their Subjects, because it is their number that preserve their Dominions, for number is strength; and it is the number of Subjects that makes a Prince great, as well as strong, by which he becomes not only able to defend his own Territories, but to Conquer others.

Secondly, to Incourage all honest ways and Arts, whereby their Poor may earn their Food; their being always more Poor, then ways to imploy them.

For in all Nations where there is property of Land, there is an hundred Poor that have nothing but their Labour to pay for their eating, to one that have either Land, Money, or Goods; for the Maintenance of life. Now if they are not imployed, they cannot pay for their eating, but are Fed gratis; then the Land that Feeds, them yields no profit, so that then it will be the same, as if there had been no property of Land; but if the Poor are imployed, the Prince and Proprietors of the Land are made Rich (that is) are Supplier, and furnished with all things necessary and convenient for the support, ease and pleasure of life, and for the Strength and Glory of a Nation.

The general imployments of the Poor, are the providing of Food, Cloaths, and Lodgings: The providing of Food doth not imploy many hands, for Ten Men are able to manage as much ground, as the product will feed two hundred; In the Clothing of a Nation many hands are imployed, but the greatest number is in providing Houses and conveniencies for their Habitations.

What those Advantages are that accrue to a Nation, by the imploying of the People, in providing of Houses and conveniencies for Habitations, and the dependancies thereon: will appear under these six heads.

First, Increase of Buildings Inrich the People.

2. They add to the Strength of a Nation.

3. They are the Glory of a Nation.

4. They are the advantage of the Prince and Governours, by Increasing their Revenews, and rendring the people more easily Governed.

5. By answering the two great Objections, which are, that Newbuildings do impoverish the City, and Depopulate the Countrey.

And Lastly, by proving that the true Cause of the Increase of Buildings is from the blessing of the Creation. Increase and Multiply, accompanied with the present Peace and Prosperity of the Government; and to suppress and discourage Builders, is to prevent the growth of a Nation. To Banish the Increase of the People, for want of Houses and Imployments, and by confining the Nation to its Infancy, while their Neighbours are growing to their full strength, is to make it a more easie Conquest to its Enemy.

First, it Inricheth the People by increasing the Arts and ways for the People to live on, for the effects of labour; and Art are Riches, for no man is supposed to imploy his time and labour without profit.

The imployment and Arts belonging to Building are many; as the Bricklayers, Carpenters, Plasterers, Masons, Glasiers, Painters, Smiths, Plummers, and many others; besides great number of day Laborers, that these several Artificers imploy; And all these get a Livelyhood and Profit by their Labour, which otherwise might have been fed by the Parish and Charity of others.

Secondly, the imployments that are occasioned by the making and providing the several materials which those several Artists make use of and the Profit that ariseth by theof selling them; as the Profit that ariseth from the Earth, to make Brick the Profit that is paid for the Timber; for the Stone, for the Iron, for the Lead, by which a great number of People are imployed as those that belong to the Quarries, Iron-works, and Mines, all which are the improvements of the Land, and turn to the advantage of the Countrey Gentlemen.

Thirdly, the several Wayes and Arts by which the People are imployed, in the furnishing these New built Houses, as the upholsterer, Pewterer, Brasier, Tin-man, Ironmonger, Potter Turnor, and a great many more Trades, besides the imployment of Digging, and Selling the Minerals and Materials which these several Artists use. All which being considered, it will appear that half the Trades, and above half the people in the Nation are imployed, and have their dependance on New-Buildings.

Fourthly, the imployments that are occasioned by Building, are the best that a People can be imployed in, and have the most advantageous effects; because they have this peculiar advantage, that the Market is never over stockt with the Goods that are made by the imploying of these hands, which often happens to all other imployments; as in making of Stuff and Cloath, and several other Comodities; by which the prices of the Goods do so much fall, when there is more made then the consumption of the people or Market can take off, that there is greater loss in those Goods that were made before, then what is gained by the imploying of the hands, in making of new; so that the profit by the Labour of the Poor is lost, and it is much the same thing as if their food had been given them gratis: But this never happens in the Building of new Houses; for the Building of New Houses raises the Rent of the Old ones; and that this is true, appears because in the ends and out-parts of all Cities and Towns Houses are of less value then they are in the middle. Now when Cities and Towns so flourish, that they incourage Builders, so that by the addition of New-buildings, those Houses that were before the ends and Out-parts of the City or Town stand nearer to the middle; then the Rents of those Houses rise in proportion, as they become nearer to the middle of the Town: and this may be seen if we examine the flourishing condition of the City of London, within this forty or fifty years by comparing the several, then ends of the Town with its present condition; As to instance in the Strand, which within this forty or fifty years was the end of the City; but now by the addition of the New buildings of Covent-Garden, Lincolnes-Inne-Fields; Clare-Market, and those towards Pickadilly and St. James; the Strand is much nearer the middle of the Town, and the Rents of the Strand since that time are more then doubled, that is, a House that was then worth but twenty pounds per Annum, is now worth fifty; And the same may be observed at the other end of the Town without Bishop-gate, For by the addition of New-buildings in Spittle-Fields, those Houses without Bishop-gate that were worth but twenty pound per Annum, are now worth thirty; and so likewise at other ends of the Town, where there has been any addition of New buildings; the like may be observed: That which further proves this, is, that the greater the Towns are, the Rents of the Houses are the dearer; as the Houses in Bristol, Exeter, York, and other great Towns, are dearer then Houses of the same dimentions in the adjoyning villages; which could not be, if the number of Houses did occasion the cheapness of them.

The reason that the Rents of Houses rise, is from the increase of Trade; and Trade is increased by their number of Inhabitants. Now the Inhabitants can not be increased without new Houses be built.

The fifth consideration of advantage is from the improvement which the Inhabitants or Traders make by living in those New built Houses: And it was this peculiar happiness and advantage which belongs to the Building and Inlarging of Cities, which made the first Founders of Cities of such Renown, and so much Deified of old: For a Company of Men by only living together, are by the exercise of several Arts and Callings, able to Feed and Cloath themselves; which if the same number of Men lived asunder, must starve, or live upon Charity of others: As for instance, if an hundred several Trades, (viz.) a Draper, a Hosier, a Millinor, a Shoomaker, a Mealman, a Butcher, a Baker, a Brewer, &c, The Draper serves the whole Ninety nine with Cloath; and for his Cloath he hath Stockings, Gloves, Shooes, Meal, Meat, and all other conveniences. Thus by the Traffick with those ninety nine, he is Fed, Cloathed, and furnished with all necessaries and conveniences; and so are all the rest Fed and Cloathed, and maintained by the Profit of Exchange one with another. Now if these men had not lived together, they could not have had this Commerce one with another; and having no other way of living, they must either have starved, or been Fed at the charge of others.

Now that it doth Inrich the Inhabitants and Traders; it doth appear further by the continuall Increasing of New-Buildings: for if the Tennants and Traders did not thrive, and maintain each other by living in these New-built Houses they could not pay their Rents; and if the Rents were not paid for those already built, it would discourage and totally put a stop to the building of New-Houses; for the Builder lays out his Money in expectation of an improvement by Rent, and it were a madness to expect Rent for new Houses; if there were none paid for those that were before built.

The Sixth great advantage that must be attributed to Cities and New-Buildings (for those advantages that are attributed to a City; the same may be to the Increasing of it, because the advantage thereby is made the greater) is, that the increasing of the Inhabitants of a City, increaseth the Emulation of the People; and Emulation increaseth Industry, and Industry Riches: There are two great Causes, of Labour and Industry, Necessity for Food and Emulation; The Necessity of Hunger makes Men Industrious, but when Hunger is Satisfied, Industry is at an end till a new provocation of Hunger makes them work again; and those People that have no other design, but to satisfie that necessity continue always miserably Poor, as it is observed in those that only work from hand to mouth; for Hunger hath Intervalls, and so hath the Labour for it, as the Proverb faith, When the Belly is fill'd the Bones are at rest. But Emulation provoaks a continued Industry, and will allow no Intervalls, or be ever satisfied: The Cobler is always indeavouring to live as well as a Shoomaker, and the Shoomaker as well as any in the Parish; so every Neighbour and every Artist is indeavouring to outvy each other, and all Men by a perpetual Industry, are strugling to mend their former condition: and thus the People grow rich, which is the great advantage of a Nation, and this benefit ariseth solely from Cities; for in a Countrey Solitude there is little Emulation, for there if a Man be Fed and Cloathed he is a Prince to himself, because there is no body by him that is better Fed and Cloathed.

The Seventh advantage by New-buildings, is that they alter way of expence, so that by the same mony expended, a greater number of People are imployed, which is a great benefit to the Nation; for those that live in the City, spend more of their Reveneue in Cloathes, then those that live in the Country. And five pounds spent in Cloathes, is of more advantage to the Nation, then twenty pounds spent in Eating and Drinking. In the Countrey the Air is sharp and provoaks hunger, and the great end of all Mens Labour there is to satisfie that craving appetite. And the pleasures of a Country life are good Eating and Driuking: but in the City the Air is thicker, and less quantity of Meat sufficeth, and not being so violently pressed by that appetite; their minds are more at leasure to gratifie ambition, which is expressed by Cloathing and furnishing of their Houses, and in the use of several other things that are invented for the Pomp and ease of life. Now he that spends five hundred pounds per Annum, if he lives in the Country he spends four in Eating and Drinking, and but one in Cloaths; whereas if he live in the City, he spends one half of his Reveneue in Cloaths, and other necessaries for his House; Now for every five pounds that is spent in Cloathing and Furnishing a House, there is above ten persons to one, that gets it by the expence of the same Money in Meat and Drink: As to instance by the making of one Suit of Cloaths how many are maintained. The Cloathier, the Spinster, Carder, Weaver, Fuller, Dresser, Draper; for Stockings the Spinster, Knitter, Hosier. For Hats, Hatmaker, Haberdasher. For Shooes, Tanner and Shoomaker. For Gloves, Leather-Dresser and Gloves. For Linen the Merchant Linen-Draper and Semstris, besides all those that are concerned for the triming with Ribbans. The Merchant for Silk, the Throster, Dier, Weaver, Milliner, and for Silk Linning, Weaver and Mercer, Besides the Button-Seller and Button-maker, Silk-man and Taylor, and several other attendant, or underworkers to those several Trades. But to the feeding of a Man there is but the Grasier, Farmer, Butcher, Mealman, Miller, Molster and Brewer, hence it appears that there is much greater advantage to a Nation, from those that live in the City, then by those that live in the Country.

The Second Arguments for New-buildings and inlarging of Towns, is, that they increase the Strength of a Nation; First, by collecting and preserving the number of Inhabitants together. Secondly, by increasing the number of People, because in Cities and Towns they propagate faster then in the Country.

Number of Subjects is the strength of a Prince, and Vis unita fortior, is most certainly true; and the greater the City or Town is the more difficult to be taken by an Enemy, provided it is as well Scituated and Fortified as a less.

For when a City is large it will require a vast Army to make the Circumference to Besiege it, besides, by the number of Inhabitants they are an Army within themselves, and ready always to defend themselves and oppose their Enemy.

2. The next is, that the people increase faster in Cities and Towns then in the Country, and number is strength. A Sedentary life, good food, and warm cloathing are the great friends to propagation; and these are the advantages of a City life; Men that live in Cities use not their bodies to so much labour as Country imployments require. And then the imployments of the Brain is better paid, for then the labour of the Body, and by being better paid they are better fed. The day Laborer hath but eighteen pence a day, when Handicraft Trades-men, as Carpenters, Bricklayers, and the like have half a Crown, others five Shillings, ten shillings a day, as the mysterie is greater, and upon this account by having better pay; they that live in the Cities are better cloathed and warmer Housed. By this means there Bodies are not so much exposed to the inconveniencies of weather, for too much heat or cold, do either too much exhaust or chill the Protifick Spirit; and that is the reason that all Creatures that live wild, do propagate in the Spring, or fall, when the Air is most temporate; and Creatures

that are kept tame, as Pigeons and Rabbets do propagate oftener then wilde, because they are better fed, less in motion, and not so much exposed to the inconveniences of weather.

The third Argument for inlarging of Cities is, that great Cities are the Glory and reputation of a Nation; the Fame and Renown of a City gives Credit and Reputation to the Citizens. A man that is born in a great City, hath more Credit by it among Forreigners, then to be born of an Ancient Family; for the former is more known to them then the latter. When Rome was in its greatness, it was accounted a very great Honour to be born a Citizen of Rome; and the greatest favour their Friends and Allies desired, was to be Free of their City.

Now Credit and Reputation are great advantages, in that they Facilitate Commerce, by enabling the people to buy Goods upon Credit, by which they readily comply with every alteration of the Market, and manage their Trades with less Stock; so that by some quick returns of the Market, they may some times pay their Creditors with the return made by his own Goods.

Another advantage the greatness of the City brings to its Inhabitants is, that it invites many strangers and travellers to see it, who spend their money in it; and are generally the best sort of Customers: how great a profit doth arise from this curious humour of seeing of Rarities is best known to the Inhabitants of Italy, some Towns there having no other subsistence then from such Guests.

The fourth argument for new Buildings and inlarging of Towns and Cities is, from the advantage they bring to the Prince and Governours by increasing the Prince's Revenue, and rendering the People more easily governed: The People that live in Cities are more easily governed, because mens estates that live in Cities are in Trade lying dispersed in several mens hands, which when ever there is any disturbance in the Government are more in danger of being lost, then if they were in-land, therefore the peace and quiet of Government is more the Interest of Citizens then of those that live in the Country.

Secondly Cities are generally under the care of a particular Governour, whose Preferment by the Government ingages him to a watchful performance of his Trust: The presence of the Governour doth easily prevent those disturbances, which were they at distance might often ruine the Government: by this Policy the Ottaman Power governs such vast Dominions, laying the Country desolate; and driving all the People into Cities and Towns.

Secondly, His Majesties Revenues are increased, as,

First, by the duty of Hearth-money, 2ly, by the customs that are paid for Timber, Boards, and Wainscoat, and Lastly by increasing of Trade in general, by which His Majesties Customs are now doubled within forty years. For the People that live in Cities are served with Commodities from other places, the Duties that are put upon these Commodities raise a great Revenue, and they are under a necessity of paying before they have their Goods, which if the People were dispersed and did not live in Cities, no such Duty could be collected.

The objections against the increase of Buildings are, First, that they ruine the Trade of the City, and thereby impoverishes it; and will in short time depopulate it.

The Second is, that they depopulate the Country by drawing the Gentry and Commonalty into those new Buildings, and thereby is occasioned the great fall of Rents in the Country.

These are two great charges and the Builders were great offenders for doing so much mischief both to City and Country, were what is objected true; But this Charge is so far from truth that the contrary, is most true, for if new Building were supprest it would certainly lessen the Trade of the City, and occasion the fall of Rents in the Country, and be the sole cause of preventing the greatness of the City, and future prosperity of the whole Nation.

And First to make it appear, that new Buildings in the Suburbs do not take away the Trade of the City.

The Trade of the City is either Whole-sail or Retail, now first that it doth not lessen the Whole-Sail Trade of the City is plain, for the Merchants and Whole-sail Trades who deal in great quantities of Commodities, are unwilling to divide their Goods into small parcels, and therefore their Customers are the Retailers: now the increase of Buyers wheresoever they live is the advantage of the Seller therefore the increase of Retailers wheresoever they live is the advantage of the Merchant, and Whole-sail Trader, it being the same thing to them whether their Customers live in the Suburbs or Citie, so they pay them for their Goods; for all Retailers wherever they live must come into the City to buy of the Merchant or Whole-sale Trades, for in the City is the Staple of all Goods, and it will and must continue there unless London Bridge be removed, and the River made navigable; hence it appears that neither the Merchant nor Whole-sail Trades suffer and prejudice by the increase of Trade and new Buildings in the Suburbs.

Secondly, the Retail Trader receives no loss by the increase of new Buildings in the Suburbs, or at least no other loss then what is ocasion'd by setting up of his Apprentice; for those that did at first set up a retail trade in the Suburbs, must be suppos'd to have serv'd their times in the City, for the Suburbs are but the Swarm of the City, So they that have since set up, have either served theirs in the City, or with a Master that did serve in the City, for no man can be supposed to venture on a Trade he hath no skill in, so that the Traders of the Suburbs were the Apprentices of the City: now it must not be reckoned a disadvantage to the Master, that his servant should set up the trade for which he paid a consideration to learn; but if it were, it is much the less if his servant set up in the suburbs then if he should take a Shop in the City, because the greater the distance he is from his Master, the less prejudice he will do by intercepting his Masters Customers; therefore none will suppose that the Retailers of the City have auy reason to complain of the new Buildings in the Suburbs upon this account, because it only afforded an opportunity to their Apprentices to set up; for the Retailers cannot drive their Trades without Shops to shew their Commodities, and if there were no more new Buildings and no Trades to be but in the city, then the Apprentices that are to come out of their times, must stay till either their Masters die or break, or by being grown very rich give over, and these things happen so seldom and the Apprentices grow out of their time so fast, that not one half of them could have places to set-up in; for it must follow that every year the seventh or eighth part of the City must die, break, or give over, and no man must continue longer to trade then seven or eight years, or else when the City is once full; there can be no room for the Apprentices to set up in, if they should all have an intention so to do, by this means after their friends have given a considerable sum of money with them for to learn a Trade, and they having been Servants for seven years, they would be in a worse condition then before, not only by the loss of time in which they might have learnt some other way to live, but being bred so long in the softness of a City life, they are now become unfit for the labour of the Country; and therefore this must not be supposed of Citizens that they having taken money with their Apprentices, to learn them their Trade should complain of a prejudice from new Buildings in the Suburbs, because otherwise a great number of Apprentices would have been under an impossibility of ever having a place to set up in: But it will plainly appear that the Citizens have no reason to complain: Such is the happiness and advantage which attends new Buildings in the Suburbs, that they do not lessen the Trade of the City but increase it.

And that this is de facto true, appears, because the Rents of the houses in the City have risen with the increase of the Suburbs: Now the Rents of Houses could not increase, if the Trade did not, but must have decreas'd if the Trade had: For the value of a House, especially for a Retail Trader is increased, as the Tenant may be supposed to have an increase of Trade by living in it. Now the Rents of the Shops and Houses in the City, though they are fallen since the Fire, are yet increased within an hundred years to treble the value; An House that was then worth but Twenty pounds per Annum, is now worth Threescore, and this will appear to be so to any that will examine the old Leases then, with this present time, which sheweth that the Trade hath increased in proportion. Now this must be occasioned by the increase of the Houses in the Suburbs, for the City was then full of Inhabitants, and could have no augmentation of Trade from its own inhabitants; that the City was then full, appears by the Bills of Mortality, which are a good calculation of the number of people; for the number that died in it every year for 40 years together, was much about the same (excepting years of great Mortality) which may be computed to be about 2500 one year with another, varying an hundred or two as the years proved more or less sickly: For in the years 1608, 1699, 1610, there died in the City 2391, 2494, 2326. And the years 1648, 1649, 1650, there died in the City 2480, 2864, 2301. Though in the same space of time, the general Bills of Mortality were increased above 2000, as in the years 1608, 1609, 610. the general Bills were 6758, 7545, 7486. And in the years 1648, 1649, 1650. the Bills were 9283, 10499, 8749. But because about the year 1650. several great Houses in the City were built into Tenements; as the Bishop of Londons and others, thereby increasing the Inhabitants, the Bills of Mortality were raised to be about 3000. and so continued for every year after, which plainly shews that the City was full, and that the raising the Rents in the City must be from the New-buildings in the Suburbs. And the reason is, because the Builders, Traders and Inhabitants of New-houses, bring more Trade to the City then the New-traders in the Suburbs take away, That is, the Trade that is occasioned by the Expences of the Carpenters, Bricklayers, Plasterers and other Artificers; the Trade by the Selling of the Materials, as Timber, Brick, Iron, Lead, &c. The Trade by the Inhabitants and Traders in these New-houses, together with the Improvements that the several Landlords make; all which do very much increase the Trade of the City; for whatsoever Improvements are made, turns to the Increase of Trade; For he that is worth five hundred Pounds, spends more in Cloth and Diet and other necessaries, then he did when he was worth but one hundred. And it will further appear, that New-buildings cannot ruine the Trade of the City, by the Re-building and Re-inhabiting of the City: For if the Objection had been true, the greatest part of the City had still layen in its Ashes: For had it been probable that Trade would not return to the City, but it might have been detained by the New-buildings without, it had discouraged men from New-building the City. Yet notwithstanding the fear it was under of removeal, and the great advantage the out parts had by entertaining it, and the difficulty there is to remove a Retail Trade from a place (most people remembring more the place, then the Man) and the great encrease of Buildings in the Suburbs ever since the Fire, yet the City hath gradually increased, as may be observed by the Bills of Mortality, and the Trade is in a manner returned; and now the City hath almost the number of its Ancient greatness, for the last years Bill, which was no Sickly year, was 2817. which wants not much of 3000. being the usual number before the Fire. By all which it appears that the City suffereth no prejudice, but receives an advantage from the Increase of Building.

The other Objection is, that it depopulates the Countrey, and this has as little in it as the former.

The Inhabitants of the Country are either Gentrey, Yeomen, or Farmer, and Grasier, or Plough-men, and Laborers, or else Workers of Wool and other Artificers.

Now if New-buildings did drain and depopulate the Countrey, of any of those Inhabitants that are the Managers and workers of the product of the Land, then it would necessarily follow, there would be less made of the Countrey Comodities; and so consequently it would appear that Corn and Cattel, Wool, Cloath, and all other of the Countrey Manufactures, would grow scarce and also dear; for dearness doth always accompany scarcity, for the value of all Comodities ariseth from the occasion and necessity there is of them; but the contrary of this is true, for there was never a greater plenty of Corn and Cattel of England, wool, and all other Manufactures then at this time, and they were never cheaper, so that there is more made then the consumption and occasion can take off; therefore there is not wanting Inhabitants in the Country to manage, and work up the produce of it, so that New buildings do not drain the Countrey of those Inhabitants. And as for the Gentry, there is no reason they should be confined to the Countrey, for if the fall of Rents be occasioned by their coming to Town; the occasion of that loss comes from themselves, and therefore the Builders not to be blamed; but the fall of Rents in the Countrey, cannot be from the Gentries coming to live in the Suburbs, with others that cannot get inployment in the Countrey; for if there are enough left in the Countrey to manage, and work up the product of the Countrey, then there can be no less. for the People must be Fed and Cloathed where ever they live; besides, by the Gentries and others coming to Town; the way of their consumption is altred as was observed before, whereby a greater number of people are imployed in the Countrey by the Gentries living in the City. For though their may be some Towns in the Countrey, wherein there may be Several Houses stand empty, and the Towns almost forsaken for want of Inhabitants, yet this doth not imploy that the New-buildings in the Suburbs do draw any of those Inhabitants away, for if the Houses themselves, had any power to attract, they would preserve their own Inhabitants; but poor People remove because their way of Lively-hood is removed, as it happens to those Towns where the Sea hath forsaken them, and to others where the Manufactures are removed; and therefore the builders are not to be blamed for providing any of these People an imployment, which otherwise must have starved, or been fed by Charity.

Now the charge of the Carriage of the Provisions and other necessaries, does not fall upon the Countrey, but the Inhabitants of the City; for if there were no more of the products of the Countrey, then would be every year consumed; the Inhabitants of the City being under a necessity of having it, because they can't live without it, would be forced to pay very dear for the fetching of it; and this is evident for Corn, and all other Victuals is alwayes deaere at London then in the Countrey; and therefore the fall of Rents in the Countrey must be ascribed to some other Cause, then New-buildings about London. That which must be the cause is, that the product of the Conntry, is greater then the Consumption; taht is, that there is more Corn, Wool and other Commodities of the Countrey, then the People can dispose of; which makes Plenty, and Plenty makes things Cheap; now the value of the Land must fall in proportion to the value of the Goods that are procured from it; that which hath occasioned it, is, that the improvements in the Conntrey, are greater then the increase of People.

The improvement of the Countrey are many, as the

drawing of Fenns, the sowing of Sanfony and other Seeds, the disparking of Parks, the inclosing of Forrests; by which there are increases of Rents made, that do equall the fall of Rents of those Counties where the improvement is made, by all which wayes, Corn, Hay, Wool, and other Manufactures, are more plentifully stored then heretofore; now there is not an increase of the People in proportion. First, because of the great Plague in which the Nation lost 200000 Souls; and Secondly, the going away of the People to New Plantations, and to improve Ireland.

The Remidies against the fall of Rents in the Countrey, were first an Act of Parliament to bring down Interest to four per Cent. Secondl, an Act for general Naturallisation. By the first, the loss of Rents would be recompenced; for if the Land in England be fallen a Fifth. That which was Twenty Pounds per Annum, is worth now but sixteen: And if sixteen Pound per Annum to be sold, would yeild as much Money as Twenty, there would be no loss: Which it would do, because four hundred Pounds can bring in but sixteen per Annum at four per Cent, which would be sooner given for sixteen Pounds per annum in Land, then it will be now given for twenty per annum. Money being now at six per Cent, because we lose one per Cent, by purchasing at 20 years purchase. By the second, the future fall of Lands would be prevented, because by a general Act of Naturallization, Foreigners would be invited to live here; and the Increase of People would occasion a consumption of the Product of Land in proportion to the Improvements.

The true cause of the Increase of New-buildings, is from the blessing of the Creation, increass and multiply accompanied with the Peace and prosperity of the Government.

That the people do increase by the ordinary course of Nature, and that there is more born then dye, I shall not need Argument to prove, to those that believe the Scripture; the History of the Creation, and of Noahs flood: For otherwise it had been impossible for the World to have been peopled. For though the Creator of the World was pleased to add long life to the Antidiluvian Patriarchs, for the more speedy peopling of the World, it being computed to be but sixteen hundred and odd years between the Creation and the Deluge, yet it was but a reasonable advantage, for in so short space of time, from the off spring of two persons, the World was very well peopled; yet after the Flood we do not read of such long life, but the World is again repeopled by Noah and his Off-spring from the natural increase of more being born then dye, so that in the space of little more then five thousand years, as is generally computed since the Flood, we by experience find a vast number of people in all parts of the known World, notwithstanding those extraordinary destructions of mankind that have been and are still made by Wars and Plague; and besides the great hindrances and designes against the blessing of the Creation, the Propagation of mankind that are practiz'd by the Turck and the Pope. The first by Castrating of the Male, the later by Claustring of vast numbers both of Male and Female; and forbidding Marriage to the whole Tribe of the Clergy, by which the encrease of a vast number of people are prevented, which later designe hath been a severer Judgement against the race of mankind in those places where it hath been Practiz'd, then either the Sword or Plague, which we may a little guess at, if we consider what a numerous Off-spring came frome Abraham by Isaac in the space of about 400 years; which was to the time the Children of Israel went out of Egypt, which were 60305 men from 20 years old and upwards, besides Women, Children; which if so great an encrease came from the Off-spring of one person, what might have been produced from the vast numbers Claustered persons since the first time of that imposition: For the promise to Abraham that his Seed should be as the sand of the Sea, did imploy, that he should have Issue, and that it should be lasting, and continue on the earth, rather then any, extraordinary and more then natural encrease from that Issue: For we do not read that the Jewish women had more Children, or that the men were longer lived then those of other Nations. And the Clergy of other Nations have showne themselves as prolifick, where they have allowed themselves Marrriage as other people.

That this matter of fact is true, that there are more born then die. Mr. Grants in his observations on the Bills of Mortality, hath undeniably proved. And the reason why the Bills of London do not shew the encrease of Christnings, is because the Dissenters to the Church of England, do not Register their Christnings, whereas all that dye are Registred; for before the Dissenters did increase, the Christnings did exceed the Burialls, as in the year 1604. the Burialls were but 5219. Whereas the Christnings were 5458. and almost every year for sometime after shewed an increase of Christnings; but as Dissenters increased, the Bills altered, as it appears after in the years 1658, and 1659. the Burrials were 14993, 15756. and the Christnings but 6170, 5690. Now it can never be supposed that there was no more borne in those years then there was fifty odd years before, seeing the people are encreased above donble the number, as it appears by the Bills, for none of the years are sickly; so that it is very evident that people do encrease. By what proportion they increase Mr. Grant hath likewise observed, by which he Calculated, that the Inhabitants within the Bills of Mortality doubled in eighty years, and those in the Countrey in two hundred and eighty.

But if we take the calculation nearer, we shall find that the people within the Bills of Mortality, have almost doubled in less then thirty years; for in the years 1648 and 1649, the Bills of Mortality were 9223, 10499, and in the years 1676, 1677, they were 18733, 19067, by which it appears that the numbers are almost doubled, nor is this increase so great, as what Mr. Grant hath observed by the Bills of Mortality of Amsterdam; for that in seven years, viz. from 1617 to 1624, there were Christned 52557, and there died in the same time but 32532; so that the Christnings did exceed the Burials 20005. Now if we allow three in one hundred according to Mr. Grant Computation; and allow 9000 to be the Increase of the Burials from the year 1650 to 1677; Then the Increase of the Inhabitants of London, will be since that time 300000. Now it is uot to be imagined that these 300000 could have continued together, if New Houses had not been built to receive them: for Houses are Hives, and without new ones the swarm would be lost, and the People would remove to some other part of the World

That the People cannot Increase their number without Increase of Houses is evident, by which hath been observed from the Bills of Mortallity of London; for that in the space of forty years together. The number was about 2500 till some Houses were built into Tenements, and after thar the Bills were about 3000.

The truth of this is yet further confirmed by the observation of the effects, that the restraining and discouraging of Builders have had upon the Nation; First, from that Act that was made in 35 of Q. Eliz. to suppress New-buildings; and Secondly, from the Act made in the late Usurper Olivers days, to charge new Foundations, the effects of both which were, that the People as fast as they did Increase, were forced to some other parts of the World for want of Houses, and the imployments that are occasioned from them, and the profit that would have risen to the Nation from their labour and consumption was lost; First, for by that Act of Parliament made in 35 of Q. Elizabeth, although it was but a Probational Act to continue till the next Session of Parliament; yet it had that influence to discourage, and restrain the Builders; that after it was expired, no man durst Build without a License; and the Parliament being sensible of the great prejudice, the suppression of Building was to a Nation; did address to His late Majesty on that behalf, as appears by my Lord Cooks Reports: Now the prejudice was very visible, for that the number of Inhabitants within the Bill of Mortalllity, did not Increase so much in the space of thirty years, as they did in the next seven years; when there was free liberty to build; for in the years 1618, 1619 and 1620, the Bills of Mortallity were 9590, 7999, 9694, and in the years 1648, 1649, and 1650, they were 9283, 10949, 9749 so that the increase of these 30 years were not a thousand, now in the year 1655, and 1657, the Burials were 11548, 13915 12430, by wich it appears, that in these next seven years the Bills were increased two thousand: now it cannot be supposed but that the People did propagate as often in those 30 years, as in the next seven years after; and therefore it must follow, that for want of Houses and imployment thereby, the People did remove to some other part of the World as fast as they Increased: Now the number of those that then removed, were not less then 300000 if the Computation be made from the Increase of the Burials of the next thirty years, as we observed before; and there is no other reason to the contrary, except that of restraining Builders. And that the People did go out of the Land is plain, for in those 30 years six Plantations were begnn (to wit.) New England, Virginia, Maryland, Barbadoes, St. Christopherus, and Bermudos, in which Plantation of New-England, some compute near an hundred thousand Families; how great an advantage, so great a number of People which are in all these Plantations would have been to the Nation, and what little profit they now yield, is apparent to every man that considers.

Secondly, the same ill consequences may be observed from that Act of Parliament, made in the late Usurper Olivers days, to charge new Foundations; which did so discourage and ruine so many Builders; that for seven years together, while the memory and fears of that Act did continue, there were no New Buildings, and the increase of the People were again driven away for want of Habitations and imploy, as appears by the Bills of Mortallity; for in the years 1656 and 1657 about which time the Act was made, the Bills were 13915, 12430, and in the years 1662 and 1663, the Bills wer 13652, 12732. About which time the Builders began to be Incouraged as appears, for St. James-Market Place, and some other part of the Town, began to be then built. So that in this space of time, there appears no Increase, though in the same space of time a little before; the Bills were Increased 2000 as we did observe; and in the next space of time after, the Bills were Increased above 3000. For in the years 1671, 1672 the Bills were 18230, 17504, which showes plainly, that the People were necessitated to remove into other parts of the world for want of Imployments and Habitations; and this appears to be true, for that great Island of Jamaica, was Planted at that time.

And that the cheif cause of the begining and growth of these Plantation, was from the suppressing and discouraging of the Builders; (though some are of opinion, that they were occasioned by the Laws against Dissenters from the Church of England) is very manifest because, if the putting those Laws in Execution, had been the Cause, there would have been as great Plantations began since; for within these 15 or 16 years, severer Laws have been made against the Dissenters, then any that were in force in those times; and yet because these hath been a liberty to Builders, no new Plantation hath since thriven: whereas, on the contrary in Oliver the late Usurpers days, though there was then liberty of Conscience, the great Plantation of Jamaica did then succeed.

Another ill conseqence of this Act made to charge new

Foundations was, that it occasioned the Rents of the land in the Country to fall.

For the number of people that were driven away in this space of these seven years, were about 100000. if the Calculation be made from the 3000. increase of the Burialls in the next seven years after.

Now the loss of those 100000, people, with the loss of the 200000. that died of the Plague in two or three years after, was the occasion of that suddain fall of Rents of Land in the Countrey, as appears plainly, for 300000 people are a twentieth part of the whole Nation, allowing six Millions of People in England and Wales, according to Mr. Grants Calculation, so that if the Land did yeild every year as much as did feed and maintaine the whole number, then the Rents of the Land must fall twelve pence in the Pound to allow for the loss of those Goods which the twentieth part of the Nation did before consume. And because, this twelve pence in the Pound was not equally divided, some Land fell a fourth and fifth to make the proportion of those that did not fail.

Thus I have shewed, that the people do increase, and that they cannot be preserved together, unless they are imployed in Building. Romulus therefore began his Government with the foundation of a City, and the States of Holland have followed the same example, to lay the foundations of the future greatness of their Government, having twice thrown down the walls of their Capital City, and at the publick charge made their Graffs and Street to encourage the Builders; and the same method have all the rest of their Cities followed, outbiding one another in their offers of Priviledges for the inlarging of them, and it hath succeeded accordingly for within the last fourscore years, since they cal'd themselves

Poor Distressed States, that Government, is thrice as Rich, Strong and great as they were before. Now, if the Building and enlarging of a City be of so great an advantage. If the employing of the poor makes a Nation Rich, if number of People make it Strong, if a great City be the Glory of a Nation, if it renders a people more easily governed, and encreases the Princes Revenue; and if it be impossible for a Nation to be either Rich, Strong or Great, without encrease of Buildings: If all this be true, that the Builders are such publick Benefactors to a Nation, it will be thought very severe that they should receive a particular Punishment for doing so much good.

FINIS.

A LETTER TO A Gentleman in the Country,

Giving an Account of the

Two Insurance-Offices;

THE

Fire-Office & Friendly-Society.

A LETTER TO

A GENTLEMAN IN THE COUNTRY,

GIVING AN ACCOUNT OF THE

TWO INSURANCE - OFFICES;

THE

FIRE-OFFICE & FRIENDLY-SOCIETY.

(1684)

A
LETTER
TO
A Gentleman in the Country,
Giving an Account of the
Two Insurance - Offices;
THE
Fire-Office & Friendly-Society.

Yours of the 15th Instant I Received; and that I might return a Satisfactory Answer, I have perused the Settlements of both the Offices: That of the Fire-Office, and that of the Friendly Society; and have sent you the Printed Papers of both, with the Observations I have made:

I. Upon the Validity of their Securities.

II. Their Interest to preserve the Insured from Fire. And

III. The Charge of Insuring.

The Fund or Securities are these: That of the Fire Office is Ground Rents [Now] to the Value of Fifty Thousand Pounds, setled upon Trustees, to make good all Losses from Fire; and to be Increased, as the Number of Houses Insured Increase.

The Strength of this Security stands upon this Supposition, That the Fund is so Large, considering the Houses Insured are dispersed at several distances, That it is very improbable (unless the whole City be Destroyed at once) that any Loss at One time should exceed the Fund; and then it will be alwayes the Interest of the Insurers (as of men that have Morgaged their Land for less than the Value) to pay the Debt when called for, to prevent a greater Loss, since the Land is of more Value than the Debt.

The Security of the Friendly Society, is the mutual Covenants between the Insured and Insurers: The Design is thus framed. The Insured deposite into the hands of the Insurers, Six Shillings, Eight Pence, for Insuring One Hundred Pound on a Brick House, and double for Timber; and Covenant to pay the residue of their Premiums when there shall be occasion, not exceeding Thirty Shillings for One Hundred Pound on a Brick House, and double on Timber, at one Loss. Upon Condition, That after such a Loss to be at Liberty to go off from the Society: Also they Covenant to pay Sixteen Pence per Annum for every Hundred Pound Insured on a Brick House, and double on Timber, for the Insurers trouble and charge of Holding Stakes, Collecting the Money, and Executing the Office, under a penalty of Losing their Money deposited; with the Benefit of being after Insured; and to be Casheired out of the Company, if they do not pay their Rent within the time limitted.

The Insurers Covenant with the Insured: And because they are Trusted with Money, give Collateral Security, to the Value of Sixteen Thousand Pounds to perform these Covenants.

1. To pay the Loss out of the Money deposited in their Hands, and Covenanted to be paid by the Insured, if it be sufficient.

2. To make a proportionable Rate, Collect the Money,

and Answer for all those that are Missing, or prove Insolvent.

3. At the end of the Term, to pay back what is left in their Hands, (except the Yearly Rent) to each of the Insured.

The Strength of this Security stands upon this Supposition, That the Premiums deposited, and agreed to be paid by the Insured, are more than sufficient to pay the Loss: And therefore there is no provision made to pay those Losses which may at one time exceed the Premiums: For the Sixteen Thousand Pounds is not Security for the Losses from Fire, but only for the Insolvent.

The Insuring of Houses being a New Design, it is impossible to make a certain guess of the Strength of this Supposition; but that I might give you some Satisfaction, I have Examined its Foundation, by Enquiring into the Profits and Loss of the Fire Office, since their first Beginning, which I find thus:

That the Fire Office in Three Years hath Insured Four Thousand Houses; And the Premiums of one House with another, do Amount to about Four pound ten shillings the House: Which in the Total, is Eighteen Thousand pounds, and they have already paid Back for Losses above Seven Thousand pounds, besides Charges.

By which it is plain, That they have Repaid almost half the Premiums, before a Fourth part of the Terms (the Houses are Insured for) are Expired: For some Houses are Insured for Seven; some for Eleven; and some for One and Twenty Years. This Calculation, any man that will Examine their Policy Books, will find to be True.

So that by what hitherto appears, its most probable, that the Premium will not be sufficient to pay the Losses; and that this Design seems to be Fram'd upon the imaginary Success of the Fire Office, incouraged by the common presumption generally believed, That men never Set Up a New Invention without

Hopes of a great advantage to themselves; and not remembring how often the first undertakers are mistaken.

But supposing the Premiums should be more then sufficient to pay the Loss; it doth not appear to me, that any man is Insured for any certain term by the Friendly Society: For how can any man be Insured for Seven years, which is a term Certain, when the number of those that are to pay the Loss is Uncertain?

1. From the Forfeiture for Non-payment of Rent.

2. From the Losses occasioning many to go off.

3. From the daily Expiration of the Terms after the first Seven years.

So that tho' the number be sufficient, when a man first Insures. By all, or any of these three Accidents, there may be too few left to pay the Loss.

And this Argument seems to me to have the greater Force, because the Fire Office that was first Set Up

Gives Better Security.

Better Preserves the Insured from Fire. And

Insures At a Cheaper Rate.

Which when Understood by those of the Friendly Society, It is reasonable to believe, many of them may alter their minds and go off.

First, The Fire Office gives Better Security, because Land was setled at first to the Value of Thirty Thousand Pounds, to make good the Loss, before a penny Premium was received; and the Premiums are setled in Proportion as the number of Houses Insured increase. But in the Friendly Society you have only the Premiums for Security.

Secondly, The Older the Fire Office, The Better; but the Friendly Society, The Older, The Worse for every Loss that happens to the Friendly Society being paid out of the Premiums, Lessens the Security: The Security is not so Large, when every man hath paid Ten or Fifteen Shillings a man towards a Loss as before: for tho by the Covenant, that a man is not at Liberty till after he hath Paid his Thirty Shillings at one Loss, the Security is the Better to Those whose Houses Are Burnt: Yet it is the Worse for Those that are Not Burnt; for they run the hazard of Losing the Value of their Houses and More, by paying Nine and Twenty Shillings a time, or less, towards Other mens Losses. Now both being Insured, it is the same thing whether their Houses be Lost by Fire, or by contributing to Others Losses.

But on the contrary, when a Loss happens to the Fire Office, It is paid out of the Bank of the Office: And the Land [which is the Fund] is never the Less; but the Older the Office grows, the Better; for as the terms of Insuring wears off, the Land is less Incumbred; and the Security is the Better to those that continue.

Secondly, In the Fire Office the Insured are better preserved from Fire, than in the Friendly Society: It is more the Interest of the Insurers: Because the Loss is their own; and experience hath already shewn, how great the advantage is to the Insured, from those Industrious men they keep to Extinguish the Fires; like Old Disciplin'd Souldiers, that do greater things, then Ten times that Number of Raw and Unexperienced men.

But in the Friendly Society, the Loss is Paid by the Insured; Therefore the Insurers cannot probably have so much damage when a Fire happens, as will equal the charge of keeping men to preserve their Houses; for they only run the hazard of paying for the Insolvent: now it is but a small sum of Money that the

Insured Covenant to pay: Who are generally owners of Houses: And the obligation not longer than for a year: (for it is not to be supposed, that the Office should pay for any after they have forfeited their Interest;) So that the Hazard is but to pay the Overplus of what is not Deposited in their Hands, if the Loss exceed it, which cannot be considerable.

But if it should; They may (as sometimes the Parish Assessors) Rate those that are Solvent something the more, to pay for those that are Insolvent: for considering the terms will daily expire. The many forfeitures and fractions, that must arise from the disproportion of the Premiums, No account can be made so plain as to discover it, or at least so easily, as to be worth any mans time to enquire into it to save a Shilling or two. So that tho those Gentlemen that now keep The Office, are men of that Known Worth and Honesty, as never to be suspected; yet by their death it may happen into such mens hands, as may gain by every Fire.

Thirdly, The Fire Office Insures at a Cheaper Rate; for in the Friendly Society, you are obliged to pay 6 s. 8 d. down for a hundred Pound in Brick, and double for Timber; and Covenant to pay your proportion of all the Losses within the term of seaven years, not exceeding Thirty Shillings per Hundred Pound, and Double for Timber for one Loss, at one time: So that if at several times the Losses amount to Ten times Thirty Shillings or more, in the Seaven years, you are obliged to pay it. And as the Chance at present appears, (by the Account of the Fire Office) it is more probable the Loss may Exceed Thirty Shillings, then be less. Therefore supposing Thirty Shillings for Seven years the medium; and Nine Shillings Four Pence for the Seaven years Rent; and Half a Crown for the Policy, makes in the Total Forty One Shillings Ten Pence, for Insuring of an Hundred Pound on a Brick House. Whereas in the Fire Office you may Insure the same sum, for the same term of years, for

Five and Twenty Shillings, and Two Shillings the Policy; which is one Third Cheaper.

To Conclude, the Friendly Society, is a more Profitable design, than the Fire Office, for the Insurers: For they have the use of about a fourth part of the Premiums; And a yearly Rent, which is better than Interest for the remainder; with the running little or no hazard.

But the Insured are just in the same Condition or rather Worse than if they had not Insured: For What ever the Loss be; It must be Paid, if ever, by the Insured, who are Owners of the Houses; And then it is the same thing whether paid by Contribution, or Parternorship, or by every mans paying singly for his own. For what is saved by the Contribution, is lost by increase of the Hazard.

For supposing that there are One Hundred Thousand Houses in this City, or within the Bills of Mortality, and One Thousand of them are Insured by the Friendly Society; It is then but a Hundred to One, when any Fire Happens, that some of the Insured Houses are Burnt. And at the same time is one Hundred Thousand to One against any particular mans House Not Insured, that it is Not Burnt; So that it is an Equal Chance, That the whole Thousand Houses Insured Are Burnt, as soon as any particular House Not Insured is Burnt: For a Thousand Hundreds to One, makes One Hundred Thousand to One. As in the Lottery of the Royal Oak, It is an equal Chance, That a Quarter Figure, which is Eight to One, should Turn Up four times, as soon as a Whole Figure once, which is two and Thirty to One. For Four Eights makes Two and Thirty.

Now to make an Instance of this Insurance; Suppose Three Hundred & Ten Brick Houses in a Town, worth, one with another, One Hundred Pound; Of which number Three Hundred Are Insured by the Friendly Society, and Ten are Not Insured: And suppose it an Equal Chance, That Ten Houses may be every year Burnt. In one Month Four Houses are Burnt, which Were Insured at Three Hundred Pounds; So that by Twenty Shillings a House, among Three Hundred, the Loss is paid. Another Month Two Houses Insured at One Hundred and Fifty Pound, are Burnt, which comes to Ten Shillings the House. And within the year, Three more. And in Seven Years and a Half, a fourth part of the Town is (by Ten Houses in a Year) Burnt and Rebuilt; And no loss at one time, did Amount to Four Hundred and Fifty Pounds, which is Thirty Shillings a House: And yet upon Stating the Account, every man hath equally Lost a Fourth part of his House: Those that were Not Burnt, by paying the Premiums, to those that Were Burnt.

And supposing the Society to continue in this Friendship Thirty one Years; The whole Number of Three Hundred and Ten Houses Are Burnt; The Ten that were Not Insured, Were Burnt: And of the Three Hundred Insured, Some were Burnt Twice; Some Thrice; And some Never Burnt: And yet there is no Difference between the Insured & Not Insured. Betwixt those that Were Burnt; And Not Burnt. For every Man Lost his House, and every Man equally Paid for the Loss. Those that were not Burnt, lost their Houses, by Paying for those that were Burnt Twice, and Thrice: Only those that were Insured Lost their Houses Yearly, by contributing Ten and Twenty Shillings at a time, towards one anothers Losses; and those Not Insured, lost their Houses at Once. But then with this Advantage all the time, They made use of their own Premiums, Saved the Rent of the Office, and Trouble of Examining Accounts.

But if the Instance be made, That the Three Hundred Houses were half Brick, and half Timber, Then the Difference will be Great; for the Timber paying Double Premium, and receiving it back Single, they will have lost their own Houses, and also have Paid for the Loss of the Brick Houses.

But the Fire Office is Much Better for the Insured; For the

Loss is paid by the Insurers, and their Land is Morgaged for the Payment: For there can be no Insurance, unless there be a Fund Setled, that is both Certain and Able to make good the Loss.

These are the Remarks I have made, to which I Expect your Answer, with your further Order about Insuring your Houses.

SIR,
Your Humble Servant,
N. B.

London, Jan. 26. 84.

AN

APOLOGY

FOR THE

BUILDER:

OR A

DISCOURSE

SHEWING THE

Cause and Effects

OF THE

INCREASE

OF

Building.

LONDON, Printed for *Cave Pullen* at the *Angel* in St. *Pauls*-Church-yard, 1685.

AN APOLOGY FOR THE BUILDER:

OR A DISCOURSE SHEWING THE

Cause and Effects

OF THE INCREASE OF

Building.

LONDON, Printed for Cave Pullen at the Angel

in St. Pauls-Church-yard

(1685)

AN APOLOGY FOR THE BUILDER

To write of Architecture and its several parts, of Situation, Platforms of Building, and the quality of Materials, with their Dimensions and Ornaments: To discourse of the several Orders of Columns, of the Tuscan, Dorick, Ionick, Corinthian, and composit, with the proper inrichments of their Capitals, Freete and Cornish, were to transcribe a Folio from Vitruvius and others; and but mispend the Readers and Writers time, since we live in an Age and Country, where all the Arts belonging to Architecture are so well known and practised: And yet at the same time and place to write an Apology for the Artist may seem a greater trifling. In a time when since the Grecian Greatness their Arts were never better performed. In a place where Buildings are generally so well finish'd, that almost every House is a little Book of Architecture; and as the ancient Artists made Athens and the rest of their Cities famous by their Buildings, and still preserve the memory of the places by the ruins of their excellent Arts: so the Artists of this Age have already made the City of London the Metropolis of Europe, and if it be compared for the number of good Houses, for its many and large Piazzas, for its richness of Inhabitants, it must be allowed the largest, best built, and richest City in the world. But such is the misfortune of Greatness to be envied. The Citizens, nay the whole Nation is astonished at the flourishing condition of this Metropolis, to see every year a new Town added to the old one; and like men affrighted are troubled with misapprehensions, and easily imposed on by the false suggestions of those that envy her Grandeur, and are angry with the Builders for making her so great.

The Citizens are afraid that the Building of new Houses will lessen the Rent and Trade of the old ones, and fancy the Inhabitants will remove on a sudden like Rats that they say run away from old Houses before they tumble.

The Country Gentleman is troubled at the new Buildings for fear they should draw away their Inhabitants, and depopulate the Country, and they want Tenants for their Land. And both agree that the increase of Building is prejudicial to the Government, and use for Argument a simile from those that have the Rickets, fansying the City to be the Head of the Nation, and that it will grow too big for the Body.

This is the Charge that is laid on the Builders: Therefore the design of this Discourse is to answer these aspersions, to remove these fears and false conceptions, by confuting these Popular Errors, and shewing that the Builder ought to be encouraged in all Nations as the chief promoter of their Welfare.

This is done by shewing the Cause of the increase of Building, and the Effects; as they relate to the City, to the Country, and to the Government.

AN APOLOGY FOR THE BUILDER:

OF THE CAUSE

The Cause of the Increase of Building is from the natural increase of Mankind, that there is more born than die. From the first blessing of the Creation, Increase and multiply, joined to the good Government of a Gracious King.

There are three things that man by nature is under a necessity to take care of, to provide food for himself, Clothes and a House. For the first, all the rest of Creation as well as man is under that necessity to take care of: For life cannot be maintained without food.

The second belongs only to man, and it is a question by some, whether it is required of him by nature, or custom, because in some Countries (and those cold) men go naked.

But as to the last, it is most certain, that Man is forced to build by nature, as all those Creatures are, whose young are born so weak (like the offspring of Mankind), that they require some time for strength after their birth, to follow their Parents, or feed themselves. Thus the Rabbit, the Fox and Lion make themselves Burrows, Kennels, and Dens to bring forth, and shelter their young, but the Mare, Cow, Sheep, &c. bring forth in the open field, because their young are able to follow them as soon as folded.

So that the natural cause of Building a House is to provide a shelter for their young; and if we examine man in his Natural condition without Arts, his Tenement differs little from the rest of Nature's Herd: The Fox's Kennel though not so large; being a lesser creature, may yet for its contrivance in its several apartments be compared with any of his Cottages: Earthen walls, and covering are the manner of both their Buildings, and the Furniture of both their Houses alike: Now as the Rabbits increase, new Burrows are made, and the Boundaries of the Warren are enlarged. So it is with Man, as he increaseth, new Houses are built, and his Town made bigger.

When Mankind is civilized, instructed with Arts, and under good Government, every man doth not dress his own meat, make his own Clothes, nor build his own House. He enjoys property of Land and Goods, which he or his Ancestors by their Arts and industry gained. These Possessions make the difference among men of rich and poor. The rich are fed, clothed, and housed by the labour of other men, but the poor by their own, and the Goods made by this labour are the rents of the rich mens Land (for to be well fed, well clothed, and well lodged, without labour either of body or mind, is the true definition of a rich man.)

Now as men differ in Estates, so they differ in their manner of living. The rich have variety of Dishes, several suits of Clothes, and larger Houses; and as their riches increase, so doth their wants, as Sir William Temple hath observed, men are better distinguished by what they want, than by what they injoy. And the chief business of Trade is the making and selling all sorts of Commodities to supply their occasions. For there are more hands imployed to provide things necessary to make up the several distinctions of men. Things that promote the ease, pleasure and pomp of life, than to supply the first natural necessities from hunger, cold, and a house only to shelter their young. Now the Trader takes care from time to time, to provide a sufficient quantity of all sorts of Goods for mans occasions, which he finds out by the Market: That is, By the quick selling of the Commodities, that are made ready to be sold. And as there are Butchers, Brewers and Cooks, Drapers, Mercers and Taylors, and a hundred more, that furnish him with food and clothes; so there are Bricklayers, Carpenters, Playsterers, and many more Traders, that build houses for him, and they make houses of the first, second, and third rate of building in proportion to the increase of the several degrees of men, which they find out by the Market, that is by letting of Houses already built: so that if it were throughly believed, that Mankind doth naturally increase; this miracle of the great increase of Houses would cease, it is therefore necessary to shew that man doth naturally increase.

This may be sufficiently proved by Sacred History, That the World was first peopled by the increase from Adam and Eve, and after the deluge repeopled by Noah and his Sons Shem, Ham, and Japhet. That the Jews began from the single stock of Abraham by Isaac, and so from Jacob; and when Moses numbred them, which was not long distance of time (being computed to be about Two hundred and sixty years from Jacob) they were above Six hundred thousand fighting men, reckoning only from Twenty years old and upward, besides Women and Children. And when numbred by David, which was about four hundred and fifty years after, they were grown a very great Nation, being Thirteen hundred thousand fighting men of Judah and Israel.

But the late Lord Chief Justice Hales in his Discourse on this subject was not contented to relye wholly on Arguments from Authority of of Holy Writ, and therefore takes other Topicks to confirm the relation of Moses concerning the beginning of the world, and the peopleing of it by a natural increase.

I. From the novity of History, That no Authentick History is older than four thousand years, and none so old as Moses of the Beginning of the World.

II. From the Chronological Account of Times. That the Assyrian, Egyptian, and Grecian Accounts are to be found out in what year of the World they began.

III. From the beginning of the ancient Kingdoms, That Rome was built by Romulus in the Seventh Olympiad, the Assyrian Monarchy began by Cyrus in 55 Olympiad, and the Grecian by Alexander in III.

IV. From the first invention of Arts, That the times of the first invention of Husbandry and making of Wine are as well known, as the later Inventions of Gun-powder and Printing.

V. From the beginning of Religions, That the time of the Inauguration of the Heathen Deities are known; As when that Jupiter, Bacchus, Ceres and Aesculapius, and the rest of them were but men of great renown, and for their Good Deeds after their death worshipped; As well as when Moses, our Saviour, and Mahomet were born.

VI. From the Decays of Humaue Nature; but how far that may be true, I leave to further inquiry.

VII. From the beginning of the Patres familias, or the first Planters of the Continents and Islands of the World; that Helen gave denomination to the Grecians called Hellenista, Pelasigus, to the Pelasgi, Latinus to the Latins, and the place called Latium, Italus to the Italians, and Italy is as much to be believed, as that the English gave name to New England in America, and the Names of the Towns there, London and New York.

VIII. From the gradual increase of Mankind; That considering the time of his first Procreation, which is agreed to be about 15 or 16 years, to the time he gives over, which is about sixty: It cannot be otherwise believed but that in the space of five and forty years he must produce a numerous off-spring: And it is no wonder amongst us; For a person to live to see some hundreds descended from his loyns.

Afterwards he comes to a particular Observation of the Increase of England by comparing the present State of it with the Survey set down in the Doomsday-Book, and makes an Instance in Gloucester-Shire, by which it appeareth, that the Inhabitants of that County since that time are greatly increased. And last of all he argueth the Increase of London from the Bills of Mortality.

These are the Arguments of the late Lord Chief Justice Hales, to prove that Mankind naturally increaseth, of which he discourseth at large in his Book of the Origination of Mankind, and therein answereth all the Objections to the contrary. And because these two last Arguments from the Survey of the Doomsday-Book, and Bills of Mortality carry with them the greatest force, for they best discover the matter of Fact as to our own Nation. I have therefore made it my business to make a scrutiny into the truth of them: As to the first, it is easie to make it appear that there is thirty times more people in England than they were in William the Conqueror's time, when the Survey was taken. And as to the latter, I shall have occasion to discourse of at large hereafter.

And if it were necessary to use any further Arguments for the proof of this Matter, they would plainly appear by comparing ancient Histories with Modern in the Descriptions they give of the Countries. As to the great Woods, the many little Governments, and the manner of the Peoples living without Arts: But not to wander over many Countries, and among several Historians I will only take the short description that Caesar giveth of our own, to shew how it differs from what it now is.

He says, "That the inner part of Britanny is inhabited by such as memory recordeth to be born in the Island: And the Maritime Coast by such as came out of Belgia, either to make Incursions or Invasions, and after the War was ended they continued in the Possessions they had gained, and were called by the name of the Cities from whence they came." It is true, he saith, "The Country is very populous and well inhabited, with Houses like unto them in Gallia.": But that must be understood as other Countries of Europe were then. It appears that in England there were many Governments and little Colonies of people, "for he reckons four Kings in the County of Kent, besides some little States. And he says, Most of the Inland people sow no Corn, but live on Milk and Flesh, clothed with skins, and having their faces painted with a blew color to the end they might seem more terrible in fight. The Britans Towns, he says, is a place ditched about to make a shelter for themselves and Cattel. And their manner of fighting was by making sudden Excursions out of the Woods, and then retiring into them for shelter." All which Descriptions shew the Country was not so populous as now.

For were there are great Woods, there is not room for Pasture or Corn, to feed Mankind: Besides they are a shelter for beasts of prey, which man as he increaseth doth every where destroy, and suffers no Flesh-eaters to live but himself, except the Dog and Cat, which he maketh tame for his use. The Lion, Wolf, and the Bear are not to be found in a populous Country; and it is the first business of all the Planters in America to destroy the wild Beasts, and the Woods, to make room for themselves to plant in.

And the reason probably of those Roman Causways, that we find in England, was to make Roads through great Woods to the several Roman Colonies; though at this time we find them in open Champaign Countries; for had the Country been so then, they would certainly have made them straiter than we now find them.

The many little Governments shew the infancy of a Country, for from single Family-government first began; those Governments were but so many families of great Men: Now the large Boundaries that so many little Governments take up in a Country, make one half of the Country useless: For men are afraid to plant or sow too near their enemies Country for fear they should lose their Harvest. Therefore the same Land cannot feed so many people as when it is under but one Government.

Besides without Arts, a great number of People cannot live together; the earth by the arts of Husbandry produceth ten times more food than it can naturally. And neither can there be any great Cities, for the Inhabitants have nothing to exchange for their food, for it is the Arts of the City which are paid for the provisions of the Country.

To conclude, nothing is so plain from ancient History as that Asia was first peopled, and (according to the Description of Moses) began about Babylon: And as Mankind increased, and the Country filled with Inhabitants; Arts were invented, and they possest more ground, till they spread themselves into Egypt, and so over Africa, and from thence into Greece, over Europe, and now Europe being full, their swarm begins to fill America.

And all the ancient Descriptions of the Countries of Europe, in the times of the Roman Greatness, are just such as are now given of America, and differs vastly from what they are now, in the number of Cities, Towns, and Arts of Inhabitants.

For were America so well peopled as Europe is, those great Countries that are possest there by the Spaniards, French, Dutch and English, some of them bigger than their own Countries in Europe, could not be so quietly held, and injoyed by not a hundredth part of the people of their own Country.

And although the valor of the Roman Soldiers, and their affected Bravery (grown as it were a fashion, and a popular Emulation) conduced much to the greatness of the Roman Empire; yet nothing promoted its success so much, and gave it such large extent as the Infancy of Europe at that time, being thinly inhabited with people, without Arts, and full of little Monarchies aud States. For had it not been so, Caesar could never have over-run Gallia, Belgia, Britany, and some part of Germany, and kept them in subjection with only ten Legions of Soldiers, which was but fifty thousand men; for we have seen within these late years much greater Armies in Belgia alone, (that is within the Seventeen Provinces, and amongst them men not inferior either in courage or skill in War, and yet have not wholly subdued one Province. And perhaps had these Forces at the same time been sent into America, they might have extended their conquest over as much ground and over as many people as Caesar did.

Nor was England so populous then as now it is; For had it been, Caesar would never at first have ventured to invade it with two Legions; and at the second time when he designed a full conquest brought over with him but five Legions, that is but five and twenty thousand men.

For although some may think from the great Armies we read of; neer two Millions of men under Cyrus and Xerxes in Asia; and of vast swarms of the Goths and Vandals in Europe, in their Invasions under King Attila and others, that the world was more populous than now, because we hear of no such numbers of late; yet if it be considered, it demonstrates only the manner of their fighting, and the infancy of the world; The want of people, and Arts, rather than that it was populous.

For the Gentiles Armies were made up after the manner of the Jews, by taking all that were able to bear Armes, reckoning from about 20 years old to sixty. For when Caesar had slain the Army of the Nervii, being about 50000 men, (a valiant people, one of the Seventeen Provinces); the old men and Women Petitioning for mercy, declared that there was not 500 men left in the whole Nation, that were able to bear Arms.

And if the King of England should reckon his Army after this manner; Of his eight Million of Subjects (as they are computed to be) there could not be less than three Millions that were able to bear Armes, which would be a greater Army than ever we read of; which must shew that the world was thin of People; since the Assyrian Empire the oldest, and therefore most populous did never raise so great a number.

And those great numbers shew that they wanted Arts; for we read that the Athenians a small but learned people baffled and destroyed all the great Army of Xerxes, reckoned by some to be Seventeen hundred thousand men; And Alexander with a small number of skilful and valiant Greeks subdued the then inhabited World.

And although the Goths and Vandals, and the Cold parts of the World made their Invasion for want of room to live in, yet that proceeded from the want of Arts.

For by Arts the Earth is made more fruitful, and by the invention of the Compass and Printing, the World is made more habitable and conversable: By the first the Countries Traffick and Exchange the Commodities they abound with, for those they want. The Timber, Pitch and Tarr of the cold Countries are Exchanged for the Wine, Brandy, and Spices of the hot. By the latter all Arts are easier discovered; By Traffick and Arts the Inhabitants of the cold Countries are better fed, better clothed, and better lodged; which make them indure the Extremities of their Climates better than formerly; and as they increase they build new Towns, inlarge their Cities, and improve their own Country; instead of invading and destroying their Neighbours.

But to return home: It is plain that the natural increase of Mankind is the cause of the increase of the City, and that there are no more Houses built every year in it, than are necessary for the growth of the Inhabitants: As will somewhat appear by the number of Apprentices made free, and Marriages every year in the City.

By the best computation that I can learn, there are no less than ten thousand Married every year in the City; which is no great number considering the number of Inhabitants: And if we should allow two Weddings in a Parish every week one with another, (there being a hundred and thirty Parishes in all) it will much exceed this proportion. Now in some Parishes there is seldom less than ten in a week. And in Dukes-place, and St. Katharine's, being priviledg'd places, there is ordinarily twenty or thirty in a week.

As to the number of Apprentices that come every year out of their time, there are not less than Nine thousand; which will not be thought too great a number, if we reckon the Houses in the City, to be about Fourscore thousand: And if the fourth part of this number be allowed for the Gentry, or those which live without Trades or Professions; and the three other parts being Sixty thousand, for Trades or Professions; and one Aprentice to every House (though in some Houses are three or four Apprentices); and that in seven years the whole number come out of their time; then in every year a seventh part of Sixty thousand, (which is about Nine thousand a year) will come out of their time. Now if Mr. Grant's Computation be right, that these Houses contain Eight persons, one with another, then there ought to be a thousand Houses at least built every year for these Nine thousand Apprentices that come out of their time, and the Ten thousand Weddings to have room to breed in. And this proportion is only sufficient to lodg them, and not for places to Trade in, for nine Traders cannot live in one House. Therefore some of their Masters, or other Traders must either die, break, or being grown too rich give over their Trades to make room for some of them to have places to Trade in, besides those that are furnish'd with places by the new Houses.

But I find Mr. Grant much mistaken in his account about the number of Inhabitants in each House in the out-parts; Perhaps it was from the rebuilding of the City with Houses more capacious and more in number. For in this last five and twenty years: the Inhabitants are now a third part more, as appeareth by the Bills of Mortality; For in the year 1660 and 1661 there died between Thirteen and fourteen thousand a year, and now there dies betwixt Twenty one and twenty two thousand a year. So that there ought to have been built above Twenty six thousand Houses in these twenty five years, which is above a thousand Houses a year to lodg this increase, which are much more than have been built in the out parts, for it appears by Mr. Morgan's Map of the City that there have not been built in this time 8000 Houses, that is not 300 Houses one year with another.

But this is certain, that there are no more Houses built every year than are occasion for; because there are Tenants for the Houses, when built, and a continuancee every year to build more. For the Builders will do as other Traders, who, when the Market is overstocked with their Commodities, and no occasion for those already made, forbear to make any more, or bring them to Market, till a new occasion requireth them. And when they find they cannot lett those already built, they will desist from building, and need no Act of Parliament to hinder them. So that we may as well complain that there is too much Cloth and Stuff made, too much Corn sowed, too many Sheep or Oxen bred, as that there are too many Houses built; too many Taylors, Shoo-makers, Bakers and Brewers, as there are too many Builders.

AN APOLOGY FOR THE BUILDER:

OF THE EFFECTS OF THE INCREASE

IN BUILDINGS, AND FIRST

AS IT RELATETH TO THE CITY

New Buildings are advantageous to a City, for they raise the Rents of the old Houses. For the bigger a Town is, the more of value are the Houses in it. Houses of the same conveniency and goodness are of more value in Bristol, Exeter and Northampton, than in the little Villages adjoyning.

Houses in the middle of a Town are of more value than those at the out ends; and when a Town happens to be increased by addition of New Buildings to the end of a Town, the old Houses which were then at the end, become nearer to the middle of the Town, and so increase in value.

Houses are of more value in Cheapside, and Cornhill, than they are in Shoreditch, White-Chappel, Old-Street, or any of the Out-parts; and the Rents in some of these Out-parts have been within this few years considerably advanced by the addition of New Buildings that are beyond them. As for instance, the Rents of the Houses in Bishopsgate-Street, the Minories, &c. are raised from fifteen or sixteen pounds Per Annum, to be now worth thirty, which was by the increase of Buildings in Spittle-Fields, Shadwells and Ratcliff-Highway. And at the other end of the Town those Houses in the Strand and Charing-Cross are worth now fifty and threescore pounds Per Annum, which within this thirty years were not Lett for above twenty pounds Per Annum, which is by the great addition of Buildings since made in St. James's, Leicester-Fields, and other adjoyning parts. But in those Our-parts where no New Buildings have been added, as in Old-Street, Grub-Street, and all that side of the City which does not increase, Houses continue much of the same value, as they were twenty years ago: And the reason of this is; because Houses are of value, as they stand in a place of Trade, and by the addition of new Buildings the place becomes to be a greater Thorough-fare, by the passing and repassing of the Inhabitants to these new Buildings.

2. They are advantageous to the City, because they increase the Trade of it: The Trade of the City is either Wholesale, or Retail. Now the New Buildings of Bloomsberry, Leicester-Fields, St. James's, Spittle-Fields, &c. are like so many new Towns for the Wholesale-Trader to Traffick in. The Inhabitants of these places do eat, wear Clothes, and furnish their Houses, and whatsoever Commoditie they use, come first from the Merchants, or Wholesale-Trader. For the City is the great Mart for Goods, from whence all other places must be furnished; so that the New Buildings are beneficial to the Wholesale Trade of the City. And it appears that they are likewise advantageous to the Retail-Traders, because they can afford to give more Rent for their old Houses, than they did formerly; for otherwise none would believe that the Tenants of Bishopsgate-street, and the Minories could subsist and pay double the Rent for their

Houses within this thirty years, had they not a better Trade in those places than formerly.

AN APOLOGY FOR THE BUILDER:

OF THE EFFECTS OF NEW BUILDINGS

AS THEY RELATE TO THE COUNTRY

New Buildings are advantageous to the Country: I. By taking off the Commodities of the Country,

The Materials of these Houses, as Stones, Bricks, Lime, Iron, Lead, Timber, &c. are all the Commodities of the Country. And whatsoever the Inhabitants of these New Houses have occasion for, either for food, Apparel, or Furniture for their Houses, are at first the growth of the Country; And the bigger the Town grows, the greater is the occasion and consumption of these Commodities, and so the greater profit to the Country.

II. New Buildings provide an habitation and livelihood for the Supernumerary and useless Inhabitants of the Country. The younger Sons of the Gentry, the Children of the Yeomen and Peasants are by these means provided with Callings, Imployments, and Habitations to exercise them in; which should they have continued in the Country, would have been burdensome, and chargeable to their Friends for want of Imployments.

For there is always Inhabitants enough left in the Country for the imployments of the Country. For if the Country wanted people, there would be a want of their Commodities, for want of hands to provide them.

Now there is as much Land Plowed, and all sorts of Grain sown, and reaped every year, as there is occasion for; and sometimes more: For the Crown in some years hath been at charge to Export it. And there is as much Wooll provided and made into Clothes and Stuffs, as the Market can take off, and so for all other Commodities of the Country.

Nay there are more of all the Country Commodities every year made than formerly: There are more Stuffs, more Clothes sent up to Gerard's and Blackwell-Hall, as appears by the Entries of those Halls; and more Sheep and Oxen sent to London, and eaten, than formerly. For there are more people in the City to be fed; so that there must be more hands in the Country to provide this greater quantity of Commodities: And the Country does increase as well as the City, as hath been already observed from the Doomsday-Book.

Therefore if the Rents of the Lands fall in the Country, it must not be ascrib'd to the New-Buildings draining their Inhabitants, but to some other occasions; Which probably may be from the great improvements that are made upon the Land in the Country, either by draining of Fens; improving of Land by Zanfoin; or other profitable Seeds; inclosing of grounds, or disparking and plowing of Parks, by which means the Markets are over stock'd and furnished at a cheaper rate than those Lands can affford, who have had no advantage from improvements: Or else the Market is removed at a greater distance, and the Lands are forced to abate in their price for the carriage; The Town perhaps is decayed, that they used to furnish, and the Trade removed to some other flourishing place at a greater distance; occasioned some times by the death or removal of some great Clothier or Trader; or some other natural obstruction of the place; as the choaking up of some Haven, and the forsaking of the Sea, which is the reason of the decay of the Cinque-Ports. These or some other occasions may make some particular mens Farms fall in value; but there is never a County in England, where the Land of the whole County doth not produce a third part more in value than it did within a 100 years, and whosoever will compare these present Rents, with what they were then, will find them generally increased. Therefore the New Buildings of this City cannot prejudice the Country, but are greatly advantageous to it.

AN APOLOGY FOR THE BUILDER:

OF THE EFFECTS OF NEW BUILDINGS

AS THEY RELATE TO THE GOVERNMENT

I. New Buildings are advantageous to the King and Government. They are instrumental to the preserving and increasing of the number of the Subjects; And numbers of Subjects is the strength of a Prince: for Houses are Hives for the People to breed and swarm in, without which they cannot increase; And unless they are provided for them from time to time in proportion to their increase, they would be forced to go into the Plantations and other Countries for habitations; and so many times become the Subjects of other Princes; but at the best the Country loseth the profit of feeding them; for they that live in a City are unskilful and unfit for Country-life; and this is the reason why so many Scotch Citizens are wandring Pedlers: and that every Town in Europe hath a Scotchman for an Inhabitant.

And that this will be the Effects will appear plainly by examining the growth of the City of London, since the Buildings have flourished, with its condition, when the Buildings were prohibited; And we cannot make a better discovery of it than by the Bills of Mortality, for it is reasonable among such a number of Mankind, such a number should die; and whether it be in such a proportion as one in three and thirty, as Mr. Grant and Sir William Petit have observed, is not not so material to this purpose; but it is a certain demonstration, That if the Burials have increased, the number of Citizens hath increased, though the proportion may be uncertain.

Now to begin the Observation from the first Bills, that were Printed, which was in the year 1606, for the space of six and seven and twenty years, we shall find very little increase in the City, for in 1606 and 1607, there died between six and seven thousand a year; and in the years 1632 and 1633 there died betwixt eight and nine thousand; Now the reason of this was the People of England were a little before that time under the same mistake, as they are generally now, and cried out against the Builders, that the City would grow too big; and therefore in the 38 of Queen Elizabeth they made a Law to prohibit Buildings in the City of London; which though it was but a probationary Act, to continue only to the next Sessions of Parliament (which was but a short time) yet its effects were long; For it frighted the Builders, and obstructed the growth of the City; and none built for thirty years after, all King James his Reign, without his Majesties License; But for want of Houses the increase of the People went into other parts of the world; For within this space of time were those great Plantations of New England, Virginia, Mariland, and Burmudas began; and that this want of Houses was the occasion is plain; For they could not build in the Country, because of the Law against Cottages. For people may get children and so increase, that had not four Acres of ground to Build on.

But the People of England at last were convinced of this popular error, and petitioned in Parliament his Majesties K. Charles the Martyr, that he would take his restraint from the

Builders; and if the next period of seven and twenty years be examined, wherein there was a greater liberty of Building, though in this space there was a great Rebellion and Civil Wars, which is a great allay to the growth of the People, yet there appeareth a much greater increase of the City of London; For in the years 1656 and 1657, the Burials were twelve and thirteen thousand,

But the flourishing condition of the City of Londen raised a new clamour against the Builders, and Oliver the Usurper glad of any pretence to raise a Tax, made use of this clamor, and laid it upon the new Foundations; but though it was an heavy and unjust Tax upon the Builders, yet he got little by it, for the whole Summ collected was but Twenty thousand Pounds clear of all charges, as appears by the Records of the Exchequer; however it had the same ill effects to stop the Builders, and growth of the City; for the People for want of Houses in that time began that great and flourishing Plantation of Jamaica.

Now if the last Period since his Majesties happy Restauration be examined, wherein the Builders have had the greatest liberty, it will appear that the Inhabitants of the City have increased more than in both of the former Periods; for the yearly Bills of Mortality are now betwixt two and three and twenty thousands, so that the City is since increased one third, and as much as in sixty years before.

This is sufficient to shew that a Nation cannot increase without the Metropolis be inlarged, and how dangerous a consequence it may be to obstruct its growth, and discourage the Builders. It is to banish the People, and confine the Nation to an Infant Estate, while the Neighbouring Nations grow to the full strength of Manhood, and thereby to render it an easie conquest to its enemies.

For the Metropolis is the heart of a Nation, through which the Trade and Commodities of it circulate, like the blood through the heart, which by its motion giveth life and growth to the rest of the Body; and if that declines, or be obstructed in its growth, the whole body falls into consumption: And it is the only symptome to know the health, and thriving of a Country by the inlarging of its Metropolis; for the chief City of every Nation in the world that flourisheth doth increase.

And if those Gentlemen that fancy the City to be the Head of the Nation, would but fancy it like the heart, they would never be afraid of its growing too big; For I never read of such a disease, that the Heart was too big for the Body. And if we are of Machiavel's opinion, this simile is the best, for he saith, that Citizens make no good Counsellors, for having raised their Fortunes by Parsimony and Industry, they are usually too severe in punishing of Vice, and too niggardly in rewarding of Vertue.

2. It is the interest of the Government, to incourage the Builders; not only because they preserve and increase the Subjects, but they provide an imploy for them, by which they are fed, and get their livelihood.

There are three great ways that the People in all Governments are imployed in: In provividing Food, Clothes, and Houses. Now those ways are most serviceable to the Government, that imploy most of the People; Those that are imployed in feeding of them, are the fewest in number: for ten men may provide food enough for a thousand: but to cloth, and build Houses for them, requireth many hands: And there is that peculiar advantage that ought to be ascribed to the Builder, that he provideth the place of birth for all the other Arts, as well as for man. The Cloth cannot be made without houses to work it in. Now besides the vast numbers of People that are imployed in digging and making the Materials, the Bricks, Stone, Iron, Lead, &c. all those Trades that belong to the furnishing of an house, have their sole dependencies on the Builders, as the Upholsterers, Chair-makers, &c.

But that which is the greatest advantage, they do not only provide a Livelihood to those that belong to the building, and furnishing of Houses, but for the Tenants of those New Houses: For the People being collected and living together in one Street, they serve and trade one with another: For Trade is nothing else but an exchange of one mans labour for another: as for instance, supposing an hundred men which lived at great distance before; some in Cornwall, others in Yorkshire, and so dispersed over all the Countries in England, live together in one Street; one is a Baker, the other a Brewer, a Shoo-maker, Taylor, &c. and so in one Trade or other the whole hundred are imployed; The Baker gets his living by making Bread for the other ninety, and so do all the rest of them; which while they were dispersed at distances, were useless, and could not serve one another, and were ready to starve for want of a Livelihood.

3. But they get not only a Livelihood, but grow rich: There ariseth an emulation among them to out-live and out-vye one another in Arts. This forceth them to be industrious, and by industry they grow rich.

4. The increasing of Buildings, and inlarging of Towns, preserveth the peace of a Nation; by rendring the People more easily governed. First it is the Builders interest of all sorts of men to preserve peace: Every man that buildeth an House, gives Security to the Government for his good behaviour. For War is the Builders ruin. The Countryman may expect to enjoy his Land again, though for a time it be laid wast; the Merchant may hide his Goods, or remove them; but when the Town is besieged, the Houses are fired, the place made desolate, and nothing is left to the Builder but ruins, the sad remembrance of his condition.

Besides, all Cities are more inclined to Peace, than the Country; the Citizens Estates are in Trade, and in Goods; many of which grow useless in War, and lye in other Peoples hands, and their Debters run away, and take Sanctuary under the Sword; And Citizens being usually rich, cannot endure the hardship of War. Next, great Cities are more easily Governed, because they are under the eye of the Prince, as generally the Metropolis is; or else under some Governour, who by his rewards from the Crown, is engaged to be very watchful in preserving the Peace; so that if they should grow factious, they are more easily corrected. Thus the Ottoman Power governs his Conquest by destroying Villages and lesser Towns, and driving the People into Capital Cities, which by the presence of some Basha are governed. Thus the King of France in his late Conquests in Flanders and Alsatia, burnt some hundreds of Villages; but Luxembourg, Strasbourg, and other great Towns are preserved. And the bigger the City, the more advantageous to the Government; for from thence they are on a sudden the better supplied with Men and Ammunition, to suppress any Rebellion, or oppose a Foreign Enemy.

Lastly, New Buildings increase his Majesties Revenues, not only by the Chimney-Money, which makes it a growing Revenue; but by the Customs paid for the Materials to build and furnish the Houses. Besides they being the cause of the increase of the City, all the increase of the Revenues from the Excise and Customs (since the Cities increase) must be ascribed to them: which are a fourth part more than they were five and twenty years ago. And the Excise is not only increased in the City, but it is so in the Country; which must not be ascribed solely to the good Management, but chiefly to the natural increase of the People. For if there be a third part more People in the City than there were five and twenty years ago, there must be a proportionable increase in the Country to provide Food and Clothes for them.

To conclude, It was upon these considerations, That by the building and inlarging of a City, the people are made great, rich, and easily governed: That those ancient and famous Governments, Thebes, Athens, Sparta, Carthage and Rome, began their Dominions, and inlarged them with their Cities; and of late the States of Holland have followed these Examples.

The Citizens of Amsterdam have thrice flung down their Walls to inlarge it; so that from a little Fisher-Town within less than 200 years it is become the third or fourth City of Europe: and the rest of their Cities have followed their Pattern; and made Grafts and Streets at the charge of the Government; endeavouring to outvie one another by giving Priviledges to incourage the Builders and Inhabitants. And these States have found the effects of it; for by this means they have changed their Style from the Poor Distressed States, (as they wrote to Queen Elizabeth) to the High and Mighty States of the United Provinces.

And if the City of London hath made such a Progress within this five and twenty years, as to have grown one third bigger, and become already the Metropolis of Europe, notwithstanding the Popular Error the Nation have been infected with, and the ill censures and discouragements the Builders have met with; had they been for this last hundred years encouraged by the Government, the City of London might probably have easily grown three times bigger than now it is.

And if we consider what the natural effects of so great a City must have been; To be furnished with such large Provisions for War suitable to its greatness; Such a vast number of Ships; being situate on an Island and Navigable River; filled with innumerable Inhabitants, of such natural courage as the English are; and to be so easily transported on a sudden with all things necessary for War, it would long before this time have been a Terror to all Europe; and now would have had the opportunity, under the Government of such a Martial Prince as now reigns, to be made the Metropolis of the World; to have caused England's Monarch to be acknowledged Lord of all the Navigable Cities and Sea-port-Towns in the World; to have made an Universal Monarchy over the Seas, an Empire no less glorious, and of much more profit, than of the Land; and of larger extent, than either Caesar's or Alexander's.

FINIS.

A

Discourse

OF

TRADE.

BY

N. B. M. D.

LONDON,

Printed by *Tho. Milbourn* for the Author, 1690.

A DISCOURSE OF TRADE

BY

N. B. M. D.

LONDON,

Printed by Tho. Milbourn

for the Author, 1690.

(1690)

THE PREFACE

The Greatness and Riches of the United Provinces, and States of Venice, Consider'd, with the little Tract of Ground that belongs to either of their Territories, sufficiently Demonstrate the great Advantage and Profit that Trade brings to a Nation.

And since the Old Ammunition and Artillery of the Grecians and Romans are grown out of Use; such as Stones, Bows, Arrows, and battering Rams, with other Wooden Engines, which were in all Places easily procured or made: And the Invention of Gunpowder hath introduced another sort of Ammunition and Artillery, whose Materials are made of Minerals, that are not to be found in all Countries; such as Iron, Brass, Lead, Salt-petre, and Brimstone; and therefore where they are wanting, must be procured by Traffick. Trade is now become as necessary to Preserve Governments, as it is useful to make them Rich.

And notwithstanding the great Influence, that Trade now hath in the Support and Welfare of States and Kingdoms, yet there is nothing more unknown, or that Men differ more in their Sentiments, than about the True Causes that raise and promote Trade.

Livy, and those Antient Writers, whose elevated Genius set them upon the Inquiries into the Causes of the Rise and Fall of Governments, have been very exact in describing the several

Forms of Military Discipline, but take no Notice of Trade; and Machiavel a Modern Writer, and the best, though he lived in a Government, where the Family of Medicis had advanced themselves to the Soveraignty by their Riches, acquired by Merchandizing, doth not mention Trade, as any way interested in the Affairs of State; for until Trade became necessary to provide Weapons of War, it was always thought Prejudicial to the Growth of Empire, as too much softening the People by Ease and Luxury, which made their Bodies unfit to Endure the Labour and Hardships of War. And therefore the Romans who made War, (the only Way to Raise & Enlarge their Dominion) did in the almost Infancy of their State, Conquer that Rich and Trading City of Carthage, though Defended by Hanibal their General, one of the greatest Captains in the World: so that, since Trade was not in those days useful to provide Magazines for Wars, an Account of it is not to be expected from those Writers. The Merchant, and other Traders who should understand the true Interest of Trade, do either not understand it, or else, lest it might hinder their private Gain, will not Discover it. Mr. Munn a Merchant, in his Treatise of Trade, doth better set forth the Rule to make an Accomplished Merchant, than how it may be most Profitable to the Nation; and those Arguments every day met with from the Traders, seem byassed with Private Interest, and run contrary to one another, as their Interest are opposite.

The Turkey-Merchants Argue against the East-India-Company, the Woollen-Draper against the Mercers, and the Upholster against the Cain-Chair-Maker; some think there are too many Traders, and Complain against the Number of Builders; others against the Number of Ale-Houses; some use Arguments for the Sole making of particular Commodities, others Plead for the Sole Trading to particular Countries: So that, if these Gentlemens Reasons might prevail in getting those

Laws they so much solicite, (which all of them Affirm, would be for the Advance of Trade, and Publick Good of the Nation) there would be but a few Trades left for the next Generation of Men to be Employ'd in, a much fewer sorts of Goods to make, and not a Corner of the World to Trade to, unless they purchase a License from them.

And how fair and convincing soever their Premises may appear for the Inlarging and Advancement of Trade, the Conclusions of their Arguments, which are for Limiting and Confining of it to Number, Persons and Places, are directly opposite to the Inlarging of it.

The Reasons why many Men have not a true Idea of Trade, is, Because they Apply their Thoughts to particular Parts of Trade, wherein they are chiefly concerned in Interest; and having found out the best Rules and Laws for forming that particular Part, they govern their Thoughts by the same NOTIONS in forming the Great BODY of Trade, and not Reflecting on the different Rules of Proportions betwixt the Body and Parts, have a very disagreeable Conception; and like those, who having learnt to Draw well an Eye, Ear, Hand, and other Parts of the Body, (being Unskilful in the Laws of Symmetry) when they joyn them together, make a very Deformed Body.

Therefore, whoever will make a true Representation of Trade, must Draw a rough Sketch of the Body and Parts together, which though it will not entertain with so much Pleasure as a well-finish't Piece, yet the Agreeableness of the Parts may be as well discern'd, and thereby such Measures taken, as may best suit the Shape of the Body.

THE CONTENTS

OF TRADE

AND

THE STOCK OR WARES OF TRADE

Trade is the Making, and Selling of one sort of Goods for another; The making is called Handy-Craft Trade, and the maker an Artificer; The Selling is called Merchandizing, and the Seller a Merchant: The Artificer is called by several Names from the sort of Goods he makes. As a Clothier, Silk-weaver, Shoo-maker, or Hatter, &c. from Making of Cloth, Silk, Shooes, or Hats; And the Merchant is distinguished by the Names of the Countrey he deals to, and is called, Dutch, French, Spanish or Turkey Merchant.

The chief End or Business of Trade, is to make a profitable Bargain: In making of a Bargain there are these things to be considered; The Wares to be Sold, the Quantity and Quality of those Wares, the Value or Price of them, the Money or Credit, by which the Wares are bought, the Interest that relates to the time of performing the Bargain.

The Stock and Wares of all Trade are the Animals, Vegitables, and Minerals of the whole Universe, whatsoever the Land or

Sea produceth. These Wares may be divided into Natural and Artificial; Natural Wares are those which are sold as Nature Produceth them; As Flesh, Fish, and Fruits, &c. Artificial Wares are those which by Art are Changed into another Form than Nature gave them; As Cloth, Calicoes, and wrought Silks, &c. which are made of Wool, Flax, Cotten, and Raw Silks.

Both these Sorts of Wares are called the Staple Commoditys of those Countreys where they chiefly abound, or are made. There are Different Climates of the Heavens, some very Hot; some very Cold, others Temperate; these Different Climates produce Different Animals, Vegitables, & Minerals. The Staples of the hot Countrey, are Spices; the Staples of the Cold, Furrs; but the more Temperate Climates produce much the same sorts of Commoditys; but by difference of the Quality or Conveniency of place where they abound, they become the Staple of each Country, where they are either best or easier acquired or exchanged: Thus, Herrings, and other Fish are the Staples of Holland; the Dutch living amongst the Water, are most naturally inclined to Fishing: English Wool being the best in the World, is the Staple of England, for the same reason. Oyles of Italy, Fruits of Spain, Wine of France, with several other sorts of Commoditys, are the Staples of their several Countrys.

Staple Commodities may be divided into Native or Forreign; the Native Staple is what Each Country doth Naturally and best produce; Forreign Staple, is any Forreign Commodity, which a Country acquires by the sole Trade to a Forreign Place, or sole possession of a particular Art; as Spices are the Staple of Holland; and the making of Glass and Paper, were the Staple of Venice.

From the Stock, or Wares of Trade, these Three Things are Observable:

1. The Native Staple of each Country is the Riches of the

Country, and is perpetual, and never to be consumed; Beasts of the Earth, Fowls of the Air, and Fishes of the Sea, Naturally Increase: There is Every Year a New Spring and Autumn, which produceth a New Stock of Plants and Fruits. And the Minerals of the Earth are Unexhaustable; and if the Natural Stock be Infinite, the Artificial Stock that is made of the Natural, must be Infinite, as Woollen and Linnen Cloth, Calicoes, and wrought Silk, which are made of Flax, Wool, Cotton, and Raw Silks.

This sheweth a Mistake of Mr. Munn, in his Discourse of Trade, who commends Parsimony, Frugality, and Sumptuary Laws, as the means to make a Nation Rich; and uses an Argument, from a Simile, supposing a Man to have 1000 l. per Annum, and 2000 l. in a Chest, and spends Yearly 1500 l. per Annum, he will in four Years time Waste his 2000 l. This is true, of a Person, but not of a Nation; because his Estate is Finite, but the Stock of a Nation Infinite, and can never be consumed; For what is Infinite, can neither receive Addition by Parsimony, nor suffer Diminution, by Prodigality.

2. The Native Staple of Each Country is the Foundation of its Forreign Trade: And no Nation have any Forreign Commodities, but what are at first brought in by the Exchange of the Native; for at the first beginning of Forreign Trade, a Nation hath nothing else to Exchange; The Silver & Gold from Spain; the Silks from Turkey, Oyls from Italy, Wine from France, and all other Forreign Goods are brought into England, by the Exchange of the English Cloth, or some other Staple of England.

3. That Forreign Staples are uncertain Wealth: Some Countries by the Sole Trade to another Country, or by the Sole Possession of some Arts, gain a Staple of Forreign Commodities, which may be as profitable as the Native, so long as they enjoy the Sole possession of that Trade or Art. But that is uncertain;

for other Nations find out the way of Trading to the same place: The Artists for Advantage, Travel into other Countries, and the Arts are discover'd. Thus Portugal had the Sole Trade of India; afterwards the Venetians got a great Share of the Trade, and now the Dutch and English, have a greater share than both: The Arts of making several sorts of Silks, were chiefly confined to Genoa, & Naples; afterward Travelled into France, since into England and Holland, and are now Practised there in as great perfection as they were in Italy; So have other Arts wander'd, as the making of Looking-Glasses from Venice into England, the making of Paper from Venice into France and Holland.

OF THE QUANTITY

AND

QUALITY OF WARES

The Quantity of all Wares are known by Weight or Measure. The Reason of Gravity is not understood, neither is it Material to this Purpose; Whether it proceeds from the Elastisity of the Air, or Weight of the utmost Spheer, or from what other Causes, its sufficient, that the ways of Trying the Weights of Bodies are perfectly discover'd by the Ballance. There are Two Sorts of Weights in Common Use, the Troy, and Averdupois.

The First are used to Weigh Goods of most Value, as Gold, Silver and Silk, &c. The Latter for Coarser, and more Bulky Goods, as Lead, Iron, &c.

There are Two Sorts of Measures, the one for Fluid Bodies, as the Bushel, Gallon and Quart, for Measuring Corn, Wine and Oyl; the other for the Measuring the Dimensions of Solid Bodies, as a Yard, Ell, &c. to Measure Cloth, Silk. &c.

The Weights and Measures of all Countries differs, but that is no Prejudice to Trade; they are all made certain by the Custom or Laws of the Place, and the Trader knows the Weight or Measure in Use, in the Place he Deals to. It is the Care of the Government, to prevent and punish the Fraud of False Weights and Measures, and in most Trading-Cities, there are Publick Weigh-Houses, and Measurers: The Fraud of the Ballance, which is from the unequal Length of the end of the Beam, is least perceivable; and therefore in Weighing Goods of Value, they usually Weigh them in both Scales.

The Qualities of Wares are known by their Colour, Sound, Smell, Taste, Make, or Shape.

The Difference in the Qualities of Wares are very difficultly distinguished; those Organs that are the proper Judges of those Differencies, do very much disagree; some Men have clearer Eyes, some more distinguishing Ears, and other nicer Noses and Tastes; and every Man having a good Opinion of his own Faculties, it is hard to find a Judge to determine which is best: Besides, those Qualities that belong to Artificial Wares, such as depend upon the Mixture, Make or Shape of them, are more difficultly discover'd: Those Wares, whose Quality are produced by the just Mixture of different Bodies, such as Knives and Razors, whose sharpness arise from the Good Temperament and Mixture of the Steel & Iron, are not to be found out, but by the Use of them: And so doth the Mixture, and well making of Hats, Cloth, and many other things.

Because the Difference in the Qualities of Wares, are so difficultly understood, it is that the Trader serves an Apprenticeship to learn them; and the Knowledge of them is called the Mystery of Trade; and in common Dealing, the Buyer is forced to rely on the Skill and Honesty of the Seller, to deliver Wares with such Qualities as he affirms them to have: It is the Sellers Interest, from the Expectation of further Dealing, not to deceive; because his Shop, the Place of Dealing, is known: Therefore, those Persons that buy of Pedlars, and Wandering People, run Great Hazard of being Cheated.

Those Wares, whose Chief Qualities consist in Shape, such as all Wearing Apparel, do not so much depend upon the Honesty of the Seller; for tho' the Trader or Maker, is the Inventor of the Shape, yet it is the Fancy and Approbation of the Buyer, that brings it into Use, and makes it pass for a Fashion.

OF THE VALUE

AND

PRICE OF WARES

The Value of all Wares arise from their Use; Things of no Us, have no Value, as the English Phrase is, They are good for nothing.

The Use of Things, are to supply the Wants and Necessities of Man: There are Two General Wants that Mankind is born with; the Wants of the Body, and the Wants of the Mind; To supply these two Necessities, all things under the Sun become useful, and therefore have a Value.

Wares, useful to supply the Wants of the Body, are all things necessary to support Life, such are in Common Estimation; all those Goods which are useful to supply the Three General Necessities of Man, Food, Clothes and Lodging; But if strictly Examined, nothing is absolutely necessary to support Life, but Food; for a great Part of Mankind go Naked, and lye in Huts and Caves; so that there are but few things that are absolutely necessary to supply the Wants of the Body.

Wares, that have their Value from supplying the Wants of

the Mind, are all such things that can satisfie Desire; Desire implys Want: It is the Appetite of the Soul, and is as natural to the Soul, as Hunger to the Body.

The Wants of the Mind are infinite, Man naturally Aspires, and as his Mind is elevated, his Senses grow more refined, and more capable of Delight; his Desires are inlarged, and his Wants increase with his Wishes, which is for every thing that is rare, can gratifie his Senses, adorn his Body, and promote the Ease, Pleasure, and Pomp of Life.

Amongst the great Variety of things to satisfie the Wants of the Mind, those that adorn Mans Body, and advance the Pomp of Life, have the most general Use, and in all Ages, and amongst all sorts of Mankind, have been of Value.

The first Effects that the Fruit of the Tree of knowledge wrought upon the Parents of Mankind, was to make them cloath themselves, and it has made the most Visible Distinction of his Race, from the rest of the Creation: It is that by which his Posterity may write Man, for no Creatures adorn the Body but Man: Beside, the decking of the Body, doth not onely distinguish Man from Beast, but is the Mark of Difference and Superiority betwixt Man and Man.

There was never any part of Mankind so wild and barbarous, but they had Difference and Degree of Men amongst them, and invented some things to shew that Distinction.

Those that Cloathed with Skins, wore the Skins of those Beasts that are most difficultly taken; thus Hercules wore a Lyons Skin; and the Ermins and Sable, are still Badges of Honour. The Degree of Quality amongst the Affricans, is known by the waste Cloth, and amongst those that go naked, by adorning their Bodies with Colours, most rare amongst them, as the Red was the Colour most in Esteem amongst the Ancient Britains.

And the most Ancient and best of Histories, the Bible,

shews, That amongst the Civilized People of the World, Ear-Rings, Bracelets, Hoods and Vails, with Changeable Suits of Apparel, were then worn: And the same Ornaments for the Body are still, and ever since have been Worn, only differing in Shapes and Fashions, according to the Custom of the Country.

The Shapes of Habits are much in use, to denote the Qualities of several men; but things rare and difficult to be obtained, are General Badges of Honour: From this Use, Pearls, Diamonds, and Precious Stones, have their Value: Things Rare are proper Ensigns of Honour, because it is Honourable to acquire Things Difficult.

The Price of Wares is the present Value; And ariseth by Computing the occasions or use for them, with the Quantity to serve that Occasion; for the Value of things depending on the use of them, the Over-pluss of Those Wares, which are more than can be used, become worth nothing; So that Plenty, in respect of the occasion, makes things cheap; and Scarcity, dear.

There is no fixt Price or Value of any thing for the Wares of Trades; The Animals, and Vegetables of the Earth, depend on the Influence of Heaven, which sometimes causes Murrains, Dearth, Famine, and sometimes Years of great Plenty; therefore, the Value of things must accordingly Alter Besides, the Use of the Mind, and not the Necessitys of the Body; and those Wants, most of them proceeding from imagination, the Mind Changeth; the things grow out of Use, and so lose their Value.

There are two ways by which the value of things are a little guessed at; by the Price of the Merchant, and the Price of the Artificer: The Price that the Merchant sets upon his Wares, is by reckoning Prime Cost, Charges and Interest.

The Price of the Artificer, is by reckoning the Cost of the Materials, with the time of working them; The Price of Time is according to the Value of the Art, and the Skill of the Artist. Some Artificers Reckon Twelve, others Fifteen, and some

Twenty, and Thirty Shillings per Week.

Interest is the Rule that the Merchant Trades by; And Time, the Artificer, By which they cast up Profit, and Loss; for if the Price of their Wares, so alter either by Plenty, or by Change of the Use, that they do not pay the Merchant Interest, nor the Artificer for his Time, they both reckon they lose by their Trade.

But the Market is the best Judge of Value; for by the Concourse of Buyers and Sellers, the Quantity of Wares, and the Occasion for them are Best known: Things are just worth so much, as they can be sold for, according to the Old Rule, *Valet Quantum Vendi potest.*

OF MONY, CREDIT

AND

INTEREST

Mony is a Value made by a Law; And the Difference of its Value is known by the Stamp, and Size of the Piece.

One Use of Mony is, It is the Measure of Value, By which the Value of all other things are reckoned; as when the Value of any thing is expressed, its said, It's worth so many shillings, or so many Pounds: Another Use of Mony is; It is a Change or Pawn for the Value of all other Things: For this Reason, the Value of Mony must be made certain by Law, or else it could not be made a certain Measure, nor an Exchange for the Value of all things.

It is not absolutely necessary, Mony should be made of Gold or Silver; for having its sole Value from the Law, it is not Material upon what Metal the Stamp be set. Mony hath the same Value, and performs the same Uses, if it be made of Brass, Copper, Tin, or any thing else. The Brass Mony of Spain, the Copper Mony of Sweeden, and Tin Farthings of England, have the same Value in Exchange, according to the Rate they are set at, and perform the same Uses, to Cast up the Value of things, as the Gold and Silver Mony does; Six Pence in Farthings will buy the same thing as Six Pence in Silver; and the Value of a thing is well understood by saying, It is worth Eight Farthings, as that it is worth Two Pence: Gold and Silver, as well as Brass, Copper and Tin Mony, change their Value in those Countries, where the Law has no Force, and yield no more than the Price of the Metal that bears the Stamp: Therefore, all Foreign Coins go by Weight, and are of no certain Value, but rise and fall with the Price of the Metal. Pieces of Eight, yield sometimes 4 sh. 6 d. 4 sh. 7 d. and 4 sh. 8 d. as the Value of Silver is higher or lower: And so doth Dollars, and all Forreign Coin, change their Value; and were it not for the Law that fixeth the Value, an English Crown Piece would now yield Five Shillings and Two Pence, for so much is the Value of it, if it were melted, or in a Foreign Country. But the chief Advantage of making Mony of Silver and Gold, is to prevent Counterfeiting; for Silver and Gold, being Metals of great Value, those who design Profit by Counterfeiting the Coin, must Counterfeit the Metals, as well as the Stamp, which is more difficult than the Stamp. There's another Benefit to the Merchant, by such Mony; for Gold and Silver being Commodities for other Uses, than to make Mony; to make Plate, Gold & Silver Lace, Silks, &c. And Coins of little Bulk, in respect of their Value, the Merchant transmits such Mony from Place to Place, in Specie, according as he finds his Advantage, by the Rise of Bulloin; though this may be a Conveniency to the Merchant, it often proves a Prejudice to the State, by making Mony scarce: Therefore, there are Laws in most Countries, that Prohibit the Transportation of Mony, yet it cannot be prevented; for in Spain, though it be Capital, yet in Two Months after the Gallions are come home, there is scarce any Silver Mony to be seen in the Country.

Some Men have so great an Esteem for Gold and Silver, that

they believe they have an intrinsick Value in themselves, and cast up the Value of every thing by them: The Reason of the Mistake, is, Because Mony being made of Gold and Silver, they do not distinguish betwixt Mony, and Gold and Silver. Mony hath a certain Value, because of the Law; but the Value of Gold and Silver are uncertain, & varies their Price, as much as Copper, Lead, or other Metals: And in the Places where they are dug, considering the smalness of their Veins, with the Charges of getting them, they do not yield much more Profit than other Minerals, nor pay the Miners better Wages for digging them.

And were it not for the Waste, made of Gold and Silver, by Plate, Lace, Silks, and Guilding, and the Custom of the Eastern Princes, to lay them up and bury them, that Half which is dug in the West, is buryed in the East. The great Quantities dug out of the Earth, since the Discovery of the West-Indies, would have so much lessened the Value, that by this time, they would not have much exceeded the Value of Tin, or Copper: Therefore, How greatly would those Gentlemen be disappointed, that are searching after the Philosopher's Stone, if they should at last happen to find it? For, if they should make but so great a Quantity of Gold and Silver, as they, and their Predecessors have spent in search after it, it would so alter, and bring down the Price of those Metals, that it might be a Question, whether they would get so much Over-plus by it, as would pay for the Metal they change into Gold and Silver. It is only the Scarcity that keeps up the Value, and not any Intrinsick Vertue or Quality in the Metals; For if the Vertue were to be considered, the Affrican that gives Gold for Knives, and Things made of Iron, would have the Odds in the Exchange; Iron being a much more Useful Metal, than either Gold or Silver. To Conclude this Objection, Nothing in it self hath a certain Value; One thing is as much worth as another: And it is time, and place, that give a difference to the Value of all things.

Credit is a Value raised by Opinion, it buys Goods as Mony doe's; and in all Trading Citys, there's more Wares sold upon Credit, then for present Mony.

There are Two Sorts of Credit; the one, is Grounded upon the Ability of the Buyer; the other, upon the Honesty: The first is called a Good Man, which implys an Able Man; he generally buys upon short Time; to pay in a Month, which is accounted as ready Mony, and the Price is made accordingly. The other is accounted an Honest Man; He may be poor; he Generally buys for three and Six Months or longer, so as to pay the Merchant by the Return of his own Goods; and therefore, the Seller relys more upon the Honesty of the Buyer, than his Ability: Most of the Retail Traders buy upon this Sort of Credit, and are usually Trusted for more than double they are worth.

In Citys of great Trade, there are publick Banks of Credit, as at Amsterdam and Venice: They are of great Advantage to Trade, for they make Payments easie, by preventing the Continual Trouble of telling over Mony, and cause a great Dispatch in Business: Publick Banks are of so great a Concern in Trade, that the Merchants of London, for want of such a Bank, have been forced to Carry their Cash to Gold-Smiths, and have thereby Raised such a Credit upon Gold-Smiths Notes, that they pass in Payments from one to another like Notes upon the Bank; And although by this way of Credit, there hath been very Vast Sums of Mony lost, not less then too Millions within five and Twenty Years, yet the Dispatch and Ease in Trade is so great by such Notes, that the Credit is still in some Measure kept up.

Therefore, it is much to be wondered at, that since the City of London is the Largest, Richest, and Chiefest City in the World, for Trade; Since there is so much Ease, Dispatch, and Safety in a Publick Bank; and since such vast Losses has Happened for want of it; That the Merchant and Traders of

London have not long before this time Addressed themselves, to the Government, for the Establishing of a Publick Bank.

The Common Objection, that a Publick Bank cannot be safe in a Monarchy, is not worth the Answering; As if Princes were not Governed by the same Rules of Policy, as States are, To do all things for the Well-fair of the Subjects, wherein their own Interest is concerned.

It is True, in a Government wholly Dispotical, whose Support is altogether in it's Millitary Forces; where Trade hath no Concern in the Affaires of the State; Brings no Revenue, There might be a Jealousy, That such a Bank might tempt a Prince to Seize it; when by doing it, he doth not Prejudice the Affairs of his Government: But in England, where the Government is not Dispotical; But the People Free; and have as great a Share in the Soveraign Legislative Power, as the Subjects of any States have, or ever had; where the Customs makes great Figures, in the Kings Exchequer; where Ships are the Bullworks of the Kingdom; and where the Flourish of Trade is as much the Interest of the King as of the People, There can be no such Cause of Fear: For, What Objections can any Man make, that his Mony in the Bank, may not be as well secured by a Law, as his Property is? Or; Why he should be more afraid of Losing his Mony, than his Land or Goods?

Interest is the Rent of Stock, and is the same as the Rent of Land: The First, is the Rent of the Wrought or Artificial Stock; the Latter, of the Unwrought, or Natural Stock.

Interest is commonly reckoned for Mony; because the Mony Borrowed at Interest, is to be repayed in Mony; but this is a mistake: For the Interest is paid for Stock: for the Mony borrowed, is laid out to buy Goods, or pay for them before bought: No Man takes up Mony at Interest, to lay it by him, and lose the Interest of it.

One use of Interest: It is the Rule by which the Trader makes up the Account of Profit and Loss; The Merchant expects by Dealing, to get more then Interest by his Goods; because of bad Debts, and other Hazards which he runs; and therefore, reckons all he gets above Inteterest, is Gain; all under, Loss; but if no more than Interest, neither Profit, nor Loss.

Another use of Interest, is, It is the measure of the Value of the Rent of Land; it sets the Price in Buying and Selling of Land: For, by adding three Years Interest more than is in the Principle, Makes the usual Value of the Land of the Country; The difference of three Year is allowed; Because Land is more certain than Mony or Stock. Thus in Holland, where Mony is at three per. Cent. by reckoning how many times three is in a Hundred Pounds, which is Thirty Three; and Adding three Years more; makes Thirty Six Years Purchase; the Value of the Land in Holland: And by the same Rule, interest being at six per Cent. in England, Land is worth but Twenty Years Purchase; and in Ireland, but Thirteen; Interest being there at Ten per Cent: so that, according to the Rate of Interest, is that Value of the Land in the Country.

Therefore, Interest in all Countrys is setled by a Law, to make it certain; or else it could not be a Rule for the Merchant to make up his Account, nor the Gentleman, to Sell his Land By.

OF THE USE

AND

BENEFIT OF TRADE

The Use of Trade is to make, and provide things Necessary: Or useful for the Support, Defence, Ease, Pleasure, and Pomp of Life: Thus the Brewers, Bakers, Butchers, Poulterers, and Cooks, with the Apothecaries, Surgeons, and their Dependencies provide Food, and Medicine for the support of Life: The Cutlers, Gun-smiths, Powder-makers, with their Company of Traders, make things for Defence; The Shoomakers Sadlers, Couch, and Chair-makers, with abundance more for the Ease of Life: The Perfumers, Fidlers, Painters, and Booksellers, and all those Trades that make things to gratifie the Sense, or delight the Mind, promote Pleasure: But those Trades that are imploy'd to express the Pomp of Life, are Infinite; for, besides those that adorn Mans Body, as the Glover, Hosier, Hatter, Semstriss, Taylor, and many more, with those that make the Materials to Deck it; as Clothier, Silk-Weaver, Lace-Maker, Ribbon-Weaver, with their Assistance of Drapers, Mercers, and Milliners, and a Thousand more: Those Trades that make the

Equipage for Servants, Trappings for Horses; and those that Build, Furnish, and Adorn Houses, are innumerable.

Thus Busie Man is imployed, and it is for his own Benefit; For by Trade, the Natural Stock of the Country is improved, the Wool and Flax, are made into Cloth; the Skins, into Leather; and the Wood, Lead, Iron and Tin, wrought into Thousand useful Things: The Over-plus of these Wares not useful, are transported by the Merchants, and Exchanged for the Wines, Oyls, Spices, and every Thing that is good of Forreign Countries: The Trader hath One Share for his Pains, and the Land-Lord the Other for his Rent: So, that by Trade, the Inhabitants in general, are not only well Fed, Clothed and Lodged; but the Richer sort are Furnished with all things to promote the Ease, Pleasure, & Pomp of Life: Whereas, in the same Country, where there's no Trade, the Land-Lords would have but Coarse Diet, Coarser Clothes, and worse Lodgings⊠ and nothing for the Rent of their Lands, but the Homage and Attendance of their Poor Bare-footed Tenants, for they have nothing else to give.

Trade Raiseth the Rent of the Land, for by the Use of several sorts of Improvements, the Land Yieldeth a greater Natural Stock; by which, the Land-lord's Share is the greater: And it is the same thing, whether his Share be paid in Mony, or Goods; for the Mony must be laid out to Buy such Good's: Mony is an Immaginary Value made by a Law, for the Conveniency of Exchange: It is the Natural Stock that is the Real Value, and Rent of the Land.

Another Benefit of Trade, is, That, it doth not only bring Plenty, but hath occasioned Peace: For the Northern Nations, as they increased, were forced from the Necessities of their Climates, to Remove; and used to Destroy, and Conquer the Inhabitants of the Warmer Climates to make Room for themselves; thence was a Proverb, Omne Malum ab Aquilone:

But those Northern People being settled in Trade, the Land by their Industry, is made more Fertile; and by the Exchange of the Nations-Stock, for Wines and Spices, of Hotter Climates, those Countries become most Habitable; and the Inhabitants having Warmer Food, Clothes, and Lodgings, are better able to endure the Extreamitys of their Cold Seasons: This seems to be the Reason, That for these Seven or Eight Hundred Years last past, there has been no such Invasions from the Northern part of the World, as used to destroy the Inhabitants of the Warmer Countries: Besides, Trade Allows a better Price for Labourers, than is paid for Fighting: So it is become more the Interest of Mankind to live at home in Peace, than to seek their fortunes abroad by Wars.

These are the Benefits of Trade, as they Relate to Mankind; those that Relate to Government, are many.

Trade Increaseth the Revenue of the Government, by providing an Imploy for the People: For every Man that Works, pay by those things which he Eats and Wears, somthing to the Government. Thus the Excise and Custom's are Raised, and the more every Man Earns, the more he Consumes, and the King's Revenue is the more Increased.

This shews the way of Determining those Controversies, about which sort of Goods are most beneficial to the Government, by their Making, or Importing: The sole difference is from the Number of hands imploy'd in making them; Hence the Importation of Raw Silk, is more Profitable to the Government than Gold, or Silver; Because there are more Hands imployd in the Throwing, and Weaving of the First; than there can be in working the Latter.

Another Benefit of Trade is, It is Useful for the Defence of the Government; It Provides the Magazines of Warr. The Guns, Powder, and Bullets, are all made of Minerals, and are wrought by Traders; Besides, those Minerals are not to be had in all Countries; The great Stock of Saltpeter is brought from the East Indies, and therefore must be Imported by the Merchant, for the Exchange of the Natives Stock.

The last Benefit is, That Trade may be Assistant to the Inlarging of Empire; and if an Universal Empire, or Dominion of very Large Extent, can again be raised in the World, It seems more probable to be done by the Help of Trade; By the Increase of Ships at Sea, than by Arms at Land: This is too large a Subject to be here Treated of; but the French King's seeming Attempt to Raise Empire in Europe, being that Common Theam of Mens Discourse, has caused some short Reflections, which will appear by Comparing the Difficulty of the one, with the Probability of the other.

The Difficulties of Raising a Dominion of very Large Extent; especially in Europe, are Many.

First, Europe is grown more Populous than formerly, and there are more Fortified Towns and Cities, than were in the time of the Roman Empire, which was the last extended Dominion; and therefore, not easily Subjected to the Power of any one Prince.

Whether Europe be grown more Populous, Solely by the Natural Increase of Mankind; There being more Born than Dye, which first Peopled the World?

Or, Whether, since the Inhabitants of Europe being Addicted to Trade, the ground is made more Fertile, and yields greater Plenty of Food; which hath prevented famine, that formerly destroy'd great Numbers of Mankind: So that no great Famines, has been taken Notice of by Historians, in these Last Three Hundred Years?

Whether by Dreining Great Bogs, Lakes, and Fens, and Cutting down vast Woods, to make Room for the Increase of Mankind, the Air is Grown more Healthy; So that Plagues, and other Epidemical Diseases, are not so destructive as formerly?

none so violent, as Procopius and Wallsingham Report, which destroyed such Vast Numbers in Italy, that there were not left Ten in a Thousand; and in other Parts of Europe, not enough alive to Bury the Dead. Whereas, the Plague in (1665) the Greatest since, did not take away the Hundredth Person in England, Holland, and other Countries, where it Raged?

Whether, since the Invention of Guns and Gun-Powder, so many Men are not slain in the Wars as formerly? Xerxes lost 260000 in one Battle against the Grecians; Alexander, destroyed 110000 of Darius's Army; Marius, slew 120000 of the Cimbri; and in great Battles, seldome less than 100000 fell: But now 20000 Men are accounted very great Slaughter.

Whether, since the Northern People have fallen on Trade, such vast Numbers, are not destroyed by Invasions?

Whether, by all those Ways, or by which of them most, Europe is grown Populous, is not Material to this Discourse: It is sufficient to shew, That the Matter of Fact is so, which does appear by comparing the Antient Histories of Countries with the Modern?

In the Antient Descriptions, the Countries are full of Vast Woods, wild Beasts; the Inhabitants barbarous, and as wild, without Arts, and the Governments are like Colonies, or Herds of People: But in the Modern, the Woods are cut down, and the Lyons, Bears, and wild Beasts destroyed; no Flesh-Eaters are left to inhabit with Man, but those Dogs and Cats that he tames for his Use: Corn grows where the Woods did, and with the Timber are built Cities, Towns and Villages; the People are Cloathed, and have all Arts among them; and those little Colonies and Families, are increased into Greàt States and Kingdoms; and the most undeniable Proof of the Increase of Mankind in England, is the Doom-Day-Book, which was a Survey taken of all the Inhabitants of England, in the Reign of William the Conquerour; by which it appears, that the

People of England are increased more than double since that time: But since the Mosaical Hypothesis of the Increase of the World, is generally believed amongst the Christians. And the late Lord Chief Justice Hales, in his Book of the Origination of Mankind, hath endeavoured to satisfie all the rest of the World. It would be misspending of Time, to use any other Topick for the further Proof thereof, than what naturally follows in this Discourse, which is from the Different Success of Arms, in the Latter and Former Ages.

In the Infancy of the World, Governments began with little Families and Colonies of Men; so that, when ever any Government arrived to greater Heighth than the rest, either by the great Wisdom or Courage of the Governor, they afterwards grew a pace: It was no Difficulty for Ninus, that was the oldest Government, and consequently, the most Populous, to begin the Assyrian Empire; nor for his Successors to continue and inlarge it: Such Vast Armies of Cyrus, Darius, Hystospis and Xerxes, the least of their Forces amounting to above 500000, could not be Resisted, when the World was but thin Peopled.

These great Armies might at first sight, seem to infer, That the World was more Populous than now; because the Armies of the greatest Princes, seldom now exceed the Number of Fifty, or Sixty Thousand Men: But the Reason of those great Numbers, was, They were not so well Skilled in Military Arts, and shew that the World was in the Infancy of its Knowledge, rather than Populous; for all that were able to bear Arms, went to the Wars: And if that were now the Custom, there might be an Army in England of above Three Million, allowing the Inhabitants to be Seven Millions; and by the same Proportion, the King of France's Country, (being four Times bigger) might raise Twelve Millions; such a Number was never heard of in this World.

The next Difficulty against the inlarging of Empire by Arms, is, That since Printing, and the Use of the Needle hath been discovered, Navigation is better known, and thence is a Greater Commerce amongst Men, the Countries and Languages are more understood, Knowledge more dispersed, and the Arts of War in all Places known; so that, Men fight more upon equal Terms than formerly; and like two Skilful Fencers, fight a long Time, before either gets Advantage.

The Assyrians & Persians Conquered more by the Number of Souldiers, than Discipline; the Grecians and Romans, more by Discipline than Number; as the World grew older, it grew wiser: Learning first flourished among the Grecians, afterwards among the Romans; and as the Latter succeeded in Learning, so they did in Empire. But now both Parties are Equally Disciplin'd and Arm'd; and the Successes of War are not so great; Victory is seldom gained without some Considerable Loss to the Conquerour.

Another Difficulty to the inlarging of Dominion by Arms, is, That the Goths Overcoming the greatest Part of Europe, did by their Form of Government, so settle Liberty, and Property of Land, that it is difficult for any Prince to Change that Form.

Whether the Goths were Part of the Ten Tribes, as some are of Opinion, and to Countenance their Conjectures, have Compared the Languages of the Inhabitants, Wales, Finland and Orchadis, and other Northern Parts (little frequented by Strangers, which might alter their Language) and find them to agree with the Hebrew in many Words and Sound, all their Speech being Guttural. This is certain, their Form of Government seems framed after the Examples of Moses's Government in the Land of Canaan, by dividing the Legislative Power, according to the Property of Land, according to that Antient Maxim, That Dominion is founded upon Property of Land. There Monarchy seems to be made by an easie Division of Land into Thirds, by a Conquering Army, setting down in Peace; the General being King, has one Third; the Colonels being the Lords, another Third; and the Captains, and other Inferiour Officers being Gentlemen, another; the Common Souldiers are the Farmers, and the Conquered are the Villains: The Legislative Power is divided amongst them, according to their Share in the Land; it being necessary that those that have Property of Land, should have Power to make Laws to Preserve it.

There seems to be but two settled Forms of Government; The Turkish, and Gothick, or English Monarchy: They are both founded upon Property of Land; in the First, the Property and Legislative Power is solely in the Prince; In the Latter, they are in both the Prince and People: The one is best fittted to raise Dominion by Armies; for the Prince must be Absolute to give Command, according to the Various Fortunes of Warr: The other is Best for Trade; for men are most industrious, where they are most free, and secure to injoy the Effects of their Labours.

All other Sorts of Government, either Aristocracy, or Democracy, where the Supream Magistrate is Elective, are Imperfect, Tumultuous, and Unsettled: For Man is Naturally Ambitious.; he inherits the same Ruleing Spirit that God gave to Adam, to Govern the Creation with: And the oftner that the Throne is Empty, the oftner will Contentions and Struggles Happen to get into it: Where deter digniori is the Rule, Warr always Ensues for the Golden Prize. Such Governments will never be without such Men as Marius and Scilla, to disturb them; nor without such a Man as Caesar to Usurp them; notwithstanding all the Contrivance for their Defence by those Polititians who seems fond of such Formes of Government.

The Gothick Government being a well fixed Form, and the People so free under it, is great hinderance to the Enlarging of Dominion; for a People under a good Government do more Vigorously Defend it: A free People have more to lose than Slaves, and their Success is better Rewarded than by any Mercenary Pay, and therefore, make a better Resistance: It was the Freedom of the Grecians and Romans that raised their Courage, and had an equal Share in raising their Empires, with their Millitary Discipline: The free City of Tyre put Alexander to more Trouble to Conquer, than all the Citys of Asia.

The People of Asia, living under a Dispotick Power, made little Resistance; Alexander subdued Libia, Phaenicia, Pamphilia, without much Opposition in his Journey to meet Darius; Egypt came under Subjection without Fighting, and so did many Countries, being willing to Change the Persian Yoak: Besides, he Fought but two Battles for the whole Persian Empire; and the Resistance of those slavish People was so weak, that he did not lose 500 Grecians in either of the Battles, tho' Darius Number far exceeded his; the one being above 260000, and the other not Forty; And there was as great Disproportion in the Slaughter; for at the Battle in Cilicia he slew 110000, and that at Arbela 40000; whereas, the Spartan, a Free People, about the same time, fought with Antipater his Vice-Roy of Macedon; and in a Fight, where neither Army exceeded 60000, slew 1012 of the Macedonians, which was more than Alexander lost in both his Battles: So great is the Difference of fighting against a Free, and a Slavish Effeminate People.

For the same Reasons, That the World is grown more Populous, That the Arts of War are more known. That the People of Europe live under a Free Government. It is as difficult to keep a Country in Subjection, as to Conquer it. The People are too Numerous to be kept in Obedience: To destroy the greatest Part, were too Bloody, and Inhuman; To Burn the Towns, and Villages, and so force the People to remove, Is to lose the greatest share in Conquest; for the People are the Riches and the Strength of the Country, And it is not much more Advantage to a Prince, to have a Title to Lands, in Terra

Incognita, As to Countries without People.

Besides, Countries and Languages being more known; And Mankind more acquainted than formerly: The Oppressed People remove into the next Country they can find Shelter in, & become the Subjects of other Governments. By such Addition of Subjects, those Governments growing stronger, are better able to Resist the Incroaches of Empire: So that, every Conquest makes the next more difficult, from the Assistance of those People before Conquered; To Transplant the Conquered into a Remote Country, as formerly, Is not to be Practised; There is now no Room, the World is so full of People.

To Conquer, and leave them Free, only paying Tribute and Homage, Is the same as not to Conquer them: For there is no Reason to expect their Submission longer, than till they are able to Resist; which will not be long before they make the same Opposition, if they continue in the same Possession; and therefore, though the Romans in the Infancy of their Government, did leave several Countries Free, as an Assistance to other Conquest; yet, when they grew stronger, they turned all their Conquest into Provinces, being the surest way to keep them from Revolting.

These are the Difficulties of inlarging Dominion at Land, but are not Impediments to its Rise at Sea: For those Things that Obstruct the Growth of Empire at Land, do rather Promote its Growth at Sea. That the World is more Populous, is no Prejudice, there is Room enough upon the Sea; the many Fortified Towns may hinder the March of an Army, but not the Sailing of Ships: The Arts of Navigation being discover'd, hath added an Unlimited Compass to the Naval Power. There needs no Change of the Gothick Government; for that best Agrees with such an Empire.

The Ways of preserving Conquests gain'd by Sea, are different from those at Land. By the one, the Cities, Towns and

Villages are burnt, to thin the People, that they may be the easier Governed, and kept into Subjection; by the other, the Cities must be inlarged, and New ones built: Instead of Banishing the People, they must be continued, in their Possession, or invited to the Seat of Empire; by the one, the Inhabitants are inslaved, by the other, they are made Free: The Seat of such an Empire, must be in an Island, that their Defence may be solely in Shipping; the same way to defend their Dominion, as to inlarge it.

To Conclude, there needs no other Argument, That Empire may be raised sooner at Sea, than at Land; than by observing the Growth of the United Provinces, within One Hundred Years last past, who have Changed their Style, from Poor Distressed, into that of High and Mighty States of the United Provinces: And Amsterdam, that was not long since, a poor Fisher-Town, is now one of the Chief Cities in Europe; and within the same Compass of Time, that the Spaniard & French have been endeavouring to Raise an Universal Empire upon the Land; they have risen to that Heighth, as to be an equal Match for either of them at Sea; and were their Government fitted for a Dominion of large Extent, and their Country separated from their Troublesome Neighbour the Continent, which would Free them from that Military Charge in defending themselves, they might, in a short Time, Contend for the Soveraignity of the Seats.

But England seems the Properer Seat for such an Empire: It is an Island, therefore requires no Military Force to defend it. Besides, Merchants and Souldiers never thrive in the same Place; It hath many large Harbours fitting for a large Dominion: The Inhabitants are naturally Couragious, as appears from the Effects of the Climate, in the Game Cocks, and Mastiff Dogs, being no where else so stout: The Monarchy is both fitted for Trade and Empire. And were there an Act for a General Naturalization, that all Forreigners, purchasing Land in England, might Enjoy the Freedom of Englishmen, It might within much less Compass of Time, than any Government by Arms at Land, arrive to such a Dominion: For since, in some Parts of Europe, Mankind is harrassed and disturbed with Wars; Since, some Governours have incroached upon the Rights of their Subjects, and inslaved them; Since the People of England enjoy the Largest Freedoms, and Best Government in the World; and since by Navigation and Letters, there is a great Commerce, and a General Acquaintance among Mankind, by which the Laws and the Liberties of all Nations, are known; those that are oppressed and inslaved, may probably Remove, and become the Subjects of England: And if the Subjects increase, the Ships, Excise and Customs, which are the Strength and Revenue of the Kingdom, will in Proportion increase, which may be so Great in a short Time, not only to preserve its Antient Soveraignty over the Narrow Seas, but to extend its Dominion over all the Great Ocean: An Empire, not less Glorious, & of a much larger Extent, than either Alexander's or Caesar's.

OF THE CHIEF CAUSES

THAT

PROMOTE TRADE

The Chief Causes that Promote Trade, (not to mention Good Government, Peace, and Scituation, with other Advantages) are Industry in the Poor, and Liberality in the Rich: Liberality, is the free Usage of all those things that are made by the Industry of the Poor, for the Use of the Body and Mind; It Relates chiefly to Man's self, but doth not hinder him from being Liberal to others.

The Two Extreams to this Vertue, are Prodigality and Covetousness: Prodigality is a Vice that is prejudicial to the Man, but not to Trade; It is living a pace, and spending that in a Year, that should last all his Life: Covetousness is a Vice, prejudicial both to Man & Trade; It starves the Man, and breaks the Trader; and by the same way the Covetous Man thinks he grows rich, he grows poor; for by not consuming the Goods that are provided for Man's Use, there ariseth a dead Stock, called Plenty and the Value of those Goods fall, and the Covetous Man's Estates, whether in Land, or Mony, becomes less worth: And a Conspiracy of the Rich Men to be Covetous, and not spend, would be as dangerous to a Trading State, as a Forreign War; for though they themselves get nothing by their Covetousness, nor grow the Richer, yet they would make the Nation poor, and the Government great Losers in the Customs and Excises that ariseth from Expence.

Liberality ought Chiefly to be Exercised in an equal Division of the Expence amongst those things that relate to Food, Cloaths, and Lodging; according to the Portion, or Station, that is allotted to every Man, with some allowance for the more refined Pleasures of the Mind; with such Distributions, as may please both sect of Philosophers, Platonist and Epicureans: The Belly must not be starved to cloath the Back-Part.

Those Expences that most Promote Trade, are in Cloaths and Lodging: In Adorning the Body and the House, There are a Thousand Traders Imploy'd in Cloathing and Decking the Body, and Building, and Furnishing of Houses, for one that is Imploy'd in providing Food. Belonging to Cloaths, is Fashion; which is the Shape or Form of Apparel.

In some places, it is fixt and certain; as all over Asia, and in Spain; but in France, England, and other places, the Dress alters; Fashion or the alteration of Dress, is a great Promoter of Trade, because it occasions the Expence of Cloaths, before the Old ones are worn out: It is the Spirit and Life of Trade; It makes a Circulation, and gives a Value by Turns, to all sorts of Commodities; keeps the great Body of Trade in Motion; it is an Invention to Dress a Man, as if he Lived in a perpetual Spring; he never sees the Autum of his Cloaths: The following of the Fashion, Is a Respect paid to the Prince and his Court, by approving his Choice in the shape of the Dress. It lyes under an ill Name amongst many Grave and Sober People, but without any Just Cause; for those that Exclaim against the Vanity of the New Fashion, and at the same time, commend the Decency of the Old one, forget that that every Old Fashion was once New, and then the same Argument might have been used against it. And if an Indian, or Stranger, that never saw any person Cloathed before, were to be Judge of the Controversy, and were to Determin upon seeing at the same time a well Drest-Courtier in the New Fashion, and another in the Old, which is accounted Decent; and a third in the Robes of an Officer, which by common Esteem, had a Reverence: It will be Two to One, against any One of the Grave Fashions; for it's only Use and Custom by which Habits become Grave and Decent, and not any particular Conveniency in the shape; for if Conveniency were the Rule of Commendation, there would arise a Question not Easily to be Determined, Whether the Spanish Garb made strait to the Body, or the loose Habit of the Turks, were to be Chosen? And therefore since all Habits are equally handsome, and hard to know which is most Convenient: The Promoting of New Fashions, ought to be Encouraged, because it provides a Livelihood for a great Part of Mankind.

The next Expence that chiefly promotes Trade, is Building, which is natural to Mankind, being the making of a Nest or Place for his Birth, it is the most proper and vible Distinction of Riches, and Greatness, because the Expences are too Great for Mean Persons to follow. It is a Pleasure fit to entertain Princes; for a Magnificent Structure doth best represent the Majesty of the Person that lives in it, and is the most lasting and truest History of the Greatness of his Person.

Building is the chiefest Promoter of Trade; it Imploys a greater Number of Trades and People, than Feeding or Cloathing: The Artificers that belong to Building, such as Bricklayers, Carpenters, Plaisterers, &c. imploy many Hands; Those that make the Materials for Building, such as Bricks, Lyme, Tyle, &c. imploy more; and with those that Furnish the Houses, such as upholsterers, Pewterers, &c. they are almost

Innumerable.

In Holland, where Trade hath made the Inhabitants very Rich, It is the Care of the Government, to Incourage the Builder, and at the Charge of the State, the Grafts and Streets are made. And at Amsterdam, they have three Times, at great Expence, Thrown down the Walls of their City, and Dreined the Boggs, to make Room for the Builder: For Houses are the Places where the Artificers make their Goods, and Merchants Sell them; and without New Houses, the Trades and Inhabitants could not Increase.

Beside, There is another great Advantage to Trade, by Enlarging of Cities; the Two Beneficial Expences of Cloathing and Lodging, are Increased; Man being Naturally Ambitious, the Living together, occasion Emulation, which is seen by Out-Vying one another in Apparel, Equipage, and Furniture of the House; whereas, if a Man lived Solitary alone, his chiefest Expence, would be Food. It is from this very Custom; If the Gentry of France Living in Cities, with the Invention of Fashion; That France, tho' a Country no way fitted for Trade, has so great a share of it: It is from Fashion in Cloaths, and Living in Cities, That the King of France's Revenues is so great, by which he is become troublesome to his Neighbours, and will always be so, while he can preserve Peace within his own Country; by which, those Fountains of Riches, may run Interrupted into his Exchequer.

OF THE CHIEF CAUSES

OF THE DECAY OF TRADE IN ENGLAND

AND FALL OF THE RENTS OF LAND

The Two Chief Causes of the Decay of Trade, are the many Prohibitions and high Interest.

The Prohibition of Trade, is the Cause of its Decay; for all Forreign Wares are brought in by the Exchange of the Native: So that the Prohibiting of any Foreign Commodity doth hinder the Making and Exportation of so much of the Native, as used to be Made and Exchanged for it. The Artificers and Merchants, that Dealt in such Goods, lose their Trades; and the Profit that was gained by such Trades, and laid out amongst other Traders, is Lost. The Native Stock for want of such Exportation, Falls in Value, and the Rent of the Land must Fall with the Value of the Stock.

The common Argument for the Prohibiting Foreign Commodities, is, That the Bringing in, and Consuming such Foreign Wares, hinders, the Making and Consuming the like sort of Goods of our own Native Make and Growth; therefore Flanders-Lace, French Hats, Gloves, Silks, Westphalia-Bacon,

&c. are Prohibited, because it is supposed, they hinder the Consumption of English-Lace, Gloves, Hats, Silk, Bacon, &c. But this is a mistaken Reason, and ariseth by not considering what it is that Occasions Trade. It is not Necessity that causeth the Consumption, Nature may be Satisfied with little; but it is the wants of the Mind, Fashion, and desire of Novelties, and Things scarce, that causeth Trade. A Person may have English-Lace, Gloves, or Silk, as much as he wants, and will Buy no more such; and yet, lay out his Mony on a Point of Venice, Jessimine-Gloves, or French-Silks; he may desire to Eat Westphalia Bacon, when he will not English; so that, the Prohibition of Forreign Wares, does not necessarily cause a greater Consumption of the like sort of English.

Besides, There is the same wants of the Mind in Foreigners, as in the English; they desire Novelties; they Value English-Cloth, Hats, and Gloves, and Foreign Goods, more than their Native make; so that, tho' the Wearing or Consuming of Forreign Things, might lessen the Consuming of the same sort in England; yet there may not be a lesser Quantity made; and if the same Quantity be made, it be a greater Advantage to the Nation, if they are Consumed in Foreign Countries, than at Home; because the Charge, and Imploy of the Freight, is Gained by it, which in bulky Goods, may be a Fourth Part of the whole Value.

The particular Trades that expect an Advantage by such Prohibition, are often mistaken; For if the Use of most Commodities depending upon Fashion, which often alters; The Use of those Goods cease. As to Instance, Suppose a Law to Prohibit Cane-Chairs; It would not necessarily follow, That those that make Turkey-Work Chairs, would have a better Trade. For the Fashion may Introduce, Wooden, Leather, or Silk Chairs, (which are already in Use amongst the Gentry, The Cane-Chairs being grown too Cheap and Common) or else, they may lay aside the Use of all Chairs, Introducing the Custom of Lying upon Carpets; the Ancient Roman Fashion; still in Use amongst the Turks, Persians, and all the Eastern Princes.

Lastly, If the Suppressing or Prohibiting of some sorts of Goods, should prove an Advantage to the Trader, and Increase the Consumption of the same sort of our Native Commodity: Yet it may prove a Loss to the Nation. For the Advantage to the Nation from Trade, is, from the Customs, and from those Goods that Imploys most Hands. So that, tho' the Prohibition may Increase, as the Consumption of the like sort of the Native; yet if it should Obstruct the Transporting of other Goods which were Exchanged for them, that Paid more Custom, Freight, or Imployed more Hands in making; The Nation will be a loser by the Prohibition: As to Instance, If Tobacco or Woollen-Cloth were used to Exchange for Westphaly-Bacon, The Nation loseth by the Prohibition, tho' it should increase the Consumption of English-Bacon; because the First, Pays more Freight, and Custom; and the Latter, Imploys more Hands. By this Ruse it appears, That the Prohibiting of all unwrought Goods, such as raw Silk, Cotton, Flax, &c. and all Bulky Goods; such as Wines, Oyls, Fruits, &c. would be a Loss to the Nation; because nothing can be sent in Exchange that Imploys fewer Hands than the First, or Pays greater Freight than the Latter.

It doth not alter the Case, If the Ballance of the Account, or all the Foreign Goods, were bought by Silver or Gold; For Silver and Gold, are Foreign Commodities; Pay but little Freight, and Imploy but few Hands in the Working; And are at First brought into England, by the Exchange of some Native Goods, and having Paid for their coming hither, must Pay for the Carriage out. It is true, That if our Serge, Stuffs, or Cloth, are Exchanged for Unmanufactured Goods, it would be a greater Advantage to the Nation, because of the difference in Number of Hands in the making of the First, and the Later.

But all Trading Countries Study their Advantage by Trade, and Know the difference of the Profit by the Exchange of wrought Goods, for unwrought: And therefore, for any Nation to make a Law to Prohibit all Foreign Goods, but such only as are most Advantageous; Is to put other Nations upon making the same Laws; and the Consequence will be to Ruine all Foreign Trade. For the Foundation of all Forreign Trade, is, from the Exchange of the Native Commodities of each Country, for one another.

To Conclude, If the bringing in of Foreign Goods, should hinder the making and consuming of the Native, which will very seldom happen; this disadvantage is not to be Remedied by a Prohibition of those Goods; but by Laying so great Duties upon them, that they may be always Dearer than those of our Country make: The Dearness will hinder the common Consumption of them, and preserve them for the Use of the Gentry, who may Esteem them, because they are Dear; and perhaps, might not Consume more of the English Growth, were the other not Imported. By such Duties, the Revenue of the Crown, will be Increased; And no Exceptions can be taken by any Foreign Prince, or Government; Since it is in the Liberty of every Government, To Lay what Duty or Imposition they please. Trade will continue Open, and Free; and the Traders, Enjoy the Profit of their Trade: The Dead Stock of the Nation, that is more than can be Used, will be Carried off, which will keep up the Price of the Native Stock, and the Rent of the Land.

The next Cause of the Decay of Trade in England, and the Fall of Rents, is, That Interest is higher in England, than in Holland, and other places of great Trade: It is at Six per Cent. in England, and at Three in Holland; For all Merchants that Trade in the same sort of Goods, to the same Ports, should

Trade by the same Interest.

Interest is the Rule of Buying and Selling: And being higher in England, than in Holland; The English Merchant Trades with a Disadvantage, because he cannot Sell the same sort of Goods in the same Port, for the same Value as the Dutch Merchant. The Dutch Merchant can Sell 100 l. worth of Goods, for 103 l. And the English Merchant must Sell the same sort, for 106 l. to make the same Account of Principal and Interest.

When Sir Thomas Gresham had almost the sole Trade of Spain, and the Turky-Company the sole Selling of Cloth into Turky, and several other places; The Difference of Interest was then, no prejudice to Trade, tho' Interest was then in England, at Eight per Cent. Because, whoe're has the sole Trade to a place, may set what Price he pleaseth upon his Goods: But now, Trade is dispersed, the same sort of Manufacture, is made in several Countries. The Dutch and English Merchants, Trade in the same sort of Goods, to the same Forreign Parts, and therefore they ought to Deal by the same Interest, which is the Measure of Trade.

Besides, And the English Merchant hath the same Disadvantage in the Return of the Goods he Buys; for the Dutch Merchant making his Return in the same sort of Goods, can under-Sell him.

By this Difference of Interest, Holland is become to be the great Magazine, and Store-House of this Part of Europe, for all sorts of Goods: For they may be laid up Cheaper in Holland, than in England.

It is impossible for the Merchant when he has Bought his Goods, To know what he shall Sell them for: The Value of them, depends upon the Difference betwixt the Occasion and the Quantity; tho' that be the Chiefest of the Merchants Care to observe, yet it Depends upon so many Circumstances, that it's impossible to know it. Therefore if the plenty of the Goods, has brought down the Price; the Merchant layeth them up, till the Quantity is consumed, and the Price riseth. But the English Merchant, cannot lay up his, but with Disadvantage; for by that time, the Price is risen so as to pay Charges and Interest at Six per Cent. the same Goods are sent for from Holland, and bring down the Price: For they are laid up there, at Three per Cent, and can therefore be Sold Cheaper.

For want of Considering this, in England, many an English Merchant has been undone; for, though by observing the Bill of Lading, he was able to make some Guess of the Stock that was Imported here; and therefore, hath kept his Goods by him for a Rise: But not knowing what Stock there was in Holland, hath not been able to sell his Goods to Profit, the same Goods being brought from thence before the Price riseth high enough to pay Ware-House-Room, and Interest.

So that, now the great part of the English Trade is driven by a quick Return, every Day Buying and Selling, according to a Bill of Rate every day Printed. By this Means, the English Trade is narrowed and confined, and the King loseth the Revenue of Importation, which he would have, if England were the Magazine of Europe; and the Nation loseth the Profit, which would arise from the Hands imploy'd in Freight and Shipping.

Interest being so high in England, is the Cause of the Fall of Rents; for Trade being confined to a Quick Return: And the Merchant being not able to lay up Foreign Goods, at the same Interest as in Holland, he Exports less of the Native; and the Plenty of the Native Stock Brings down the Rent of Land; for the rest of the Land that produceth the Stock, must fall, as the Price of the Stock doth.

Whereas, if Interest were at the same Rates as in Holland, at Three per Cent. it would make the Rent more certain, and raise the Value of the Land.

This Difference of Three per Cent. is so Considerable, that

many Dutch Merchants Living in Holland, having Sold their Goods in England; give Order, to put out their Stock to Interest in England; thinking That a better Advantage than they can make by Trade.

It will raise the Rent of some Estates, and preserve the Rent of others: For the Farmer must make up his Account, as the Merchant doth; the Interest of the Stock, must be reckoned, as well as the Rent of Land: Now if the Farmer hath 300 l. Stock, upon his Farm, that is so easily Rented, that he Lives well upon it; he may add 9 l. per Annum more to the Rent, when the Interest is at Three per Cent. and make the same Account of Profit from the Farm: As he doth now Interest, is at Six per Cent. And those Farmers that are hard Rented, having the same Stock, will have 9 l. per Annum Advance in the Account, towards the Easing the Rent: For altho' the Farmer gets nothing more at the Years end, yet in making up of Account, there must 9 l. add to the Value of Land, and taken from the Account of the Stock. If Interest were at Three per Cent. there would always be a Magazine of Corn and Wooll in England, which would be a great Advantage to the Farmer, and make his Rent more certain; for there are Years of Plenty, and Scarcity; and there are more Farmers undone by Years of great Plenty, than Recover themselves in Years of Scarcity; for when the Price is very low, the Crop doth not Pay the Charge of Sowing, Farming, and Carrying to Market; and when it is Dear, It doth not fall to all Mens Fortune that were losers by Plenty, to have a Crop: Now if Interest were at Three per Cent. Corn and Wooll in Years of great Plenty, would be Bought and Laid up to be Sold in Years of Scarcity. The Buying in Years of Plenty, would keep the Price from Falling too Low; and the Selling in Years of Scarcity, would prevent it from Rising too High; by this means, a moderate Price, being best upon Corn and Wooll; the Farmers Stock and Rent of the Land, would be more certain.

But now Holland being the great Magazine of Corn, Man will Lay up any considerable Quantity in England at Six per Cent. when he may always Buy as much as he wants, that was Laid up at Three per Cent. and may bring it from thence, as Soon, and as Cheap, into any Parts of England, as if it were Laid up here.

Thirdly, If Interest were at Three per Cent. the Land of England, would be worht from Thirty Six, to Forty Years Purchase; for Interest, sets the Price in the Buying and Selling of Land.

The bringing down of Interest, will not alter the Value of other Wares; for the Value of all Wares, arriveth from their Use; and the Dearness and Cheapness of them, from their Plenty and Scarcity: Nor will it make Mony more Scarce. For if the Law allow no more Interest, than Three per Cent. they that Live upon it, must Lend at that rate, or have no Interest; for they cannot put it forth any where else to better Advantage. But if it be supposed, That it may make Mony scarce, and that it may be a Prejudice to the Government, who want the Advance of the Mony; It may be provided for, by a Clause, that all that Lend Mony to the King, shall have 6 l. per Cent.; such Advantage would make all Men Lend to the Government: And the King will save two per Cent. by such a Law.

The seeming Prejudice from such a Law, is, It will lessen the the Revenue of those who live upon Interest: But this will not be a General Prejudice; for many of those Persons, have Land as well as Mony, and will get as much by the Rise of one, as the by the Fall of the other. Besides, many of them, are Persons that live Thriftily, and much within the Compass of their Estates; and therefore, will not want it, but in Opinion. They have had a long Time, the Advantage of the Borrower; for the Land yielding but 4l. per Cent. and the Interest being at 6l.

per Cent. a new Debt is every Year contracted of 2l. per Cent. more than the Value of the Debt in Land will pay, which hath Devoured many a good Farm; and eat up the Estates of many of the Ancient Gentry of England.

Moses, that Wise Law-Giver, who designed, that the Land, divided amongst the Jews, should continue in their Families; forbid the Jews to pay Interest, well knowing that the Merchants of Tyre, who were to be their near Neighbours, would, by Lending Mony at Interest, at last get their Lands: And that this seems to be the Reason, is plain; For the Jews might take Interest of Strangers, but not pay; for by taking Interest, they could not lose their Estates.

The Lawyers have invented Intails, to preserve Estates in Families; and the bringing down of Interest to Three per Cent. will much help to continue it; because the Estates being raised to double the Value, will require double the Time, after the same Proportion of Expence to Consume it in.

The raising the Value of Land, at this Time, seems most necessary, when the Nation is Engaged in such a Chargeable War: For the Land is the Fund that must support and preserve the Government; and the Taxes will be lesser and easier payd; for they will not be so great: For 3sh. in the Pound, is now 133½ Part of every Mans Estate in Land, reckoning at Twenty Years Purchase. But if the Value of the Land be doubled, it will be the 226 Part of the Land, which may be much easier born.

Campinella, who Wrote an 100 years since, upon considering of the great Tract of the Land of France; says That if ever it were United under one Prince, it would produce so great a Revenue; It might give Law to all Europe.

The Effect of this Calculation, Is since, seen by the Attempts of this present King of France: And therefore, since England is an Island, and the Number of Acres cannot be In creased; It seems absolutely necessary, That the Value of them, should be raised to Defend the Nation against such a Powerful Force: It will be some Re-compence to the Gentry, whose Lands must bear the Burthen of the VVar, to have the Value of their Estates Raised; which is the Fund and Support of the Government; Is a great Advantage to the whole Nation; and it's the greater, because it doth not Disturb, Lessen, nor Alter the Value of any Thing else.

FINIS.

AN ANSWER

To a PAPER Entituled,

REASONS *against Reducing Interest to Four* per Cent.

AN ANSWER TO A PAPER

ENTITULED,

REASONS AGAINST REDUCING INTEREST

TO FOUR PER CENT.

(1694)

AN ANSWER TO A PAPER

ENTITULED,

REASONS AGAINST REDUCING INTEREST

TO FOUR PER CENT.

Had the Author of that Paper read the Letter to a Friend against Usurie, he might have observed his own Reasons much better urged, and as well answered by Sir Tho. Culpeper Seventy Years since, being the time when Interest was reduced from Ten to Eight, which might have prevented both our Repetitions.

But since he either did not read the Letter, or was not satisfied with the Answers, it will not be a greater mispence of time to answer the Reasons, than it was again to write them.

His first Reason against Reducing Interest from Six to Four is, That it will obstruct and hinder Trade; for many Traders borrow Money at Interest to carry on their Trade; and he supposes that no Man will lend Money to Tradesmen upon personal Security, but that all Men will keep their Moneys by them for better Advantage.

But the Reason why any Man should keep his Money, and expect a better Advantage, when the Law has reduced Interest to 4 per Cent. more than now it is at 6 per Cent. he doth not give.

For why should any Man lock up his Money, rather than take 4 per Cent. It is no contemptible Interest. It is more than Land produceth? And what greater Advantage can any Man then expect, unless it be to lay it out upon Trade? If so, it will rather promote Trade, than obstruct or hinder it; and therefore it is used by Sir Tho. Culpeper, and others that have wrote on that Subject, for an Argument for the Lowering of Interest, because it will promote and increase Trade: As it is evident in those Countries, viz. in Holland and Italy, where Money is at 3 per Cent. Trade flourishes, but in Spain, and other places where the Interest of Money is at 10 and 12 per Cent. the People are poor, and have but little Trade.

His second Argument is, That the reducing of Interest to 4 per Cent. will sink the real Value of the Principle one Third; So that every Man whose Estate is in Money, would, by such a Law, loose a Third part of it, which he believes to be as great a Hardship, as to take away a Third part of every Man's Land of Inheritance: But this is a great Mistake; for the Lowering of the Interest a Third, will not lessen the Value of the Principal; for a 100 l. will buy as much Goods (and of some sort more) after such a Law is made, as it will now; It will buy as much Corn, Wool, Cloth, and all things else, except Land: It is true, a 100 l. will not buy so much Land by one Third, as it did before; for 5 l. a Year in Land of Inheritance being now worth 100 l. will then be worth 150 l. and there is the greatest Reason and Justice that it should be so; for then the Exchange will be even betwixt Land, Money, or Goods; for why should any Man give 6 per Cent. for Money or Goods, when the Land will bring in but Four? Why should a Gentleman pay 2 per Cent. more for all the Goods he buyes of the Merchant, to wit, for Cloth, Silks, Linnen, &c. more than the Merchant gives for his Wool and Corn; for the Money that Gentlemen pay Interest for, is laid out to pay for Goods they use; so that Money is but the Rent of wrought Stock, as Corn and Wool is the Rent of the Land. And it is much to be wondered at, that since the Nobility and Gentery, having the greatest share in the Legislative-Power, should not have given themselves the leisure, before this time, to have reflected upon this great Odds in the Exchange, and have made a Law to regulate the Balance. It would have prevented many large Farms and noble Mannors to have been devoured by Taylors, Mercers, and other Traders.

His third Argument is, That if Interest be reduced, it will be a prejudice to Widowes, Orphans, and others, whose whole Estates are in Money; for that the Interest of their Portion or Moneys will not be sufficient to maintain them; those that have Threescore Pounds a Year for a Thousand Pounds, will then have Forty: This is the only Objection of moment that ever I have heard of against this Law; yet if it be consider'd, it hath not that Force nor Pitty in it as it seems at first sight to have; first they are few in number in respect of the whole Nation; next, as to the Orphans, their Portions in Money will be of the same Esteem, and of the same Value to buy every thing, except Lands, and they were never given them with that intent; for then their Parents might as well have given them Lands: So that it is only the Income of the Portions that is lessened, and that is but for a short time; till the young Men set up their Trades, or till the Maidens or Widowes marry; and if in the interim they spend Ten Pounds a Year less, the first may perhaps make better Tradesmen or Merchants, and the latter make better Wives; Thrift and good Housewifery will do neither of them harm.

But this will not be the Case neither, for the Lowering of

Interest does Chiefly fall upon Foreign Stock or Wares, and the Merchant may afford to sell his Goods Two per Cent. cheaper, and will get as much by them as he did when Money was at Six per Cent. and Three parts in Four of every Gentleman's Expence is in Foreign Wares, either in Wine, Spices, Silks, Linnen, and other Manufactures; in such Goods there will be Two per Cent. saved in the Price; so that they may then maintain themselves almost as well with Forty Pounds a Year, as they do now with Threescore.

Fourthly, If Interest be reduced to Four per Cent. a greater part of the Inheritance of Gentlemens Estates that have Daughters, will be lessen'd and more incumbred; Because, he supposing the the Value of the Principal Money being sunk, they must give greater Portions: But this is grounded upon a Mistake which is before answered; for a Thousand Pounds will be as much valued by a Trader as it is now, and every Gentleman will be better able to provide Portions for his younger Children, because his Land will yield a Third part more in value: so that the Gentleman's Estate in Lands of Inheritance will be less incumbred than before.

Fifthly, If Interest be reduced to Four per Cent. it will make Money scarce, as he believes, and be only advantageous to Scriveners, who will have more for Procuration and Continuation. If this should happen, though there is no reason for it, yet the Borrower may afford to give more to the Scrivener; when he pays less to the Userer. But why any Man should believe Money should be scarce, when such a Law doth not lessen the Money, though it does the Interest. But the contrary is most true, the Lowering of Interest will make Money more plentiful; for a low Interest increaseth Trade, and Trade increaseth Money; for Bullion is a Foreign Commodity, and brought in by Trade.

The last Argument is, That the lowering of Interest will not raise the Rent of the Land; and although, as he confesseth, it will raise the Value of Land in Sale, yet the Value of Money being thereby lessened, as he conceives, there will be a necessity of greater Portions for younger Children; so that the Gentry will have no advantage by such a Law. This is a greater Mistake than all the rest; for the Rent of the Land will be raised as well as the Price; for the Interest of the Stock must be reckoned to make up the Rent of the Land. So that the takeing of Two per Cent. from the Stock, being added to the Rent of the Land, so much is the Rent of the Land raised. A Farm that is now worth Fifty Pounds per Annum, and requires Three Hundred Pounds Stock, will be worth Fifty Six Pounds per Annum, when Interest is reduced to Four per Cent. there being Six Pounds a Year taken from the Stock and added to the Rent.

To conclude, No Law can be of greater Advantage to the Nation, than the Law that will reduce Interest from Six to Four per Cent. It will produce the most general Good with the least private Disadvantage; and it being so early proposed this Session in the Honourable the House of Commons, and so often taken notice of in the Printed Votes, it was believed by most without Doors, that it was designed by the Wisdom of this present Parliament, as a Law to make some recompence for those great Taxes and heavy Impositions which the necessity of the publick Affairs require them to lay on the People. And since the Advantages of this Law hath been all over the Nation generally debated, there seems no Law, by the general Suffrage of the People, that will be more welcome, or that can make them a more general Satisfaction for such great Taxes.

FINIS

A

DISCOURSE

Concerning

Coining the New Money lighter.

IN

Anſwer to Mr. *Lock*'s Conſidera tions about raiſing the Value of Money.

By NICHOLAS BARBON, Eſq;.

LONDON

Printed for Richard Chiſwell, at the *Roſe* and *Crown* in St. *Paul's* Church-Yard. MDCXCVI.

A

DISCOURSE CONCERNING COINING

THE NEW MONEY LIGHTER.

IN ANSWER TO MR. LOCK'S CONSIDERATIONS

ABOUT RAISING THE VALUE OF MONEY.

BY

NICHOLAS BARBON, Esq.

LONDON: Printed for Richard Chiswell, at the Rose and Crown in St. Paul's Church-Yard. MDCXCVI.

(1696)

PREFACE

This Question, Whether it is for the Interest of England, at this time, to New-Coin their Clipt-Money, according to the Old Standard both for Weight and Fineness, or to Coin it somewhat Lighter? has been, of late, the business of the Press, and the common subject of Debate.

And since there has been so much wrote and said Pro & Con about this matter, and yet Gentlemen continue still unsatisfied, and of different Opinions; I could not hope, from any thing I might write, to have better success, and therefore did not intend to appear in Publick in this Controversy: Tho' I had the same reason which is given for answering Mr. Lowndes; that is, that by my silence I might seem to renounce my own Opinion, having some time since wrote a Discourse of Trade, wherein the definition of Money differs from what Mr. Lock asserts.

But having consider'd the fatal consequence of coining the Money by the old Standard, and that it was not necessary that those Argumeuts that should be offered to prevent it, should wholly convince those that are of the contrary Opinion; but that they would have the same success, if they did but create a Doubt. It seeming very reasonable, that Persons in Doubt of their own Opinion in this Controversy, might be persuaded to consent to the trial of the contrary; not only that they might thereby discover the Truth, but because by the Experiment there appears so plain an Advantage, as the multiplying the species of the Coin, and saving the Nation near a Million of Money, in a time when they are engaged in so chargeable a War.

I was therefore encouraged, in hopes of such success, to offer my Reasons, for raising the Value of the Money, to Publick Consideration, that they might be the better weigh'd and examin'd, and at the same time to answer Mr. Lock's Objections to the contrary: which, both from the Reputation of the Person that writes them, and the Reception they seem to have had from great Personages before they were published, are of greatest force in this Debate.

That which seems to be the greatest difficulty in clearing this Controversy is, That it being about a matter where Profit accompanies the decision of it, Gentlemen are jealous of the Arguments, lest they should be biass'd by private Interest, and so run contrary to the Truth: which lessens the force of the Arguments that are used in such Debates.

But this is an equal Objection to the Reason on both sides: For as the raising the Value of the Money may be profitable to those that have Interest in Banks, having great Cashes in Old Money; so on the other hand, the Coining of the Money to the Old Standard, may be as profitable to Banks by melting of it down; and if there be any difference of Advantage, it must be to the latter: Because, besides the Profit by melting, Nothing can be of greater Advantage to Banks than scarcity of Money, when men will be glad to take a Bank-Note for want of it. And on the contrary, nothing can be more disadvantageous to Banks, especially to those young in Credit, than plenty of New Money, when the Money may be sooner told than a Note writ: so that if I were to consider my private Interest, I ought to be of the contrary Opinion to that I argue for.

And therefore I hope I shall be believ'd, when I declare

that I have no other design in writing this Discourse, than the service of my Countrey; and I have the same Candor to believe it of those that have wrote for the contrary Opinion; and that Mr. Lock and I do in this agree, tho' in our Arguments we differ. For I cannot believe that any Person, for his own private Interest, will argue for the Coining the Money by the Old Standard, when the Consequence of it, in my Opinion, will be so fatal to his Countrey; which will be no less than the want of the species of Money, a stop of Trade, and a general Complaint and Poverty all over the Nation.

I have followed the same Method in answering Mr. Lock, as he has used in answering Mr. Lownds; which is, by laying down several Propositions contrary to Mr. Lock's, and from thence to argue and shew wherein his are mistaken.

I have chose rather to sum up the chief substance of his Arguments for the sake of Brevity, than to recite his sense in his own words. And if in any place I have mistaken his sense, I do beg his pardon, and do assure him that it was not wilfully, but for want of right understanding of it: For I have the same design as Mr. Lock, That Truth betwixt us might appear; and therefore shall use his own words, That I shall think my self oblig'd to him, or any one else, who shall shew me, or the Publick, any material mistake in any thing I have here said, whereon any part of the Question turns.

The want of leisure from other Affairs, might very well have been pleaded for not writing in this Debate: But if it may be allow'd me for an Excuse in not writing so well on this Subject as the weightiness of it might require, either in respect of the Stile, the Method of arguing, or the omission of several things to the clearing the Controversy, I shall not think my time ill spent, especially if any thing that I have wrote, may tend to the service of the Publick.

THE CONTENTS,

OR,

CHIEF SUBSTANCE

OF MR. LOCK'S BOOK.

That Silver is the Instrument and Measure of Commerce by its Intrinsick Value.

The Intrinsick Value of Silver is the Estimate which common consent hath placed on it.

Silver is the Measure of Commerce by its Quantity, which is also the Measure of its Intrinsick Value. It is the Quantity of Silver men give, take, and contract for, that they Estimate the Value of other things by, and give and take in exchange for all other Commodities.

That Money differs from Uncoined Silver only in this, That the Quantity of Silver in each Piece is ascertained by its stamp; which is set there to be a Publick Voucher for its Weight and Fineness.

That the Par of Money is a certain number of Pieces of the

Coin of one Countrey, containing in them an equal Quantity of Silver to that in another number of pieces of the Coin of another Countrey.

That plenty of Money in a Countrey is only made and preserved by the Ballance of Trade.

From these Propositions Mr. Lock argues,

> That it will be no Advantage to raise the Value of the Money, but a great Loss to all the Creditors and Landed Men of England.
>
> For Bullion or Uncoined Silver having an Intrinsick Value, can never rise nor fall: And money differing only from Silver in this, That the Stamp ascertains the weight and fineness of the Silver in the money, Silver can never be of a higher price than the money: For an equal Quantity of Silver will always be of the same value to an equal Quantity of Silver.
>
> That if the value of the money be rais'd, the value of all Goods will rise accordingly. For Silver being the Measure of Commerce by its Quantity; and it is the Quantity of Silver that men contract for in selling their Goods; if there be a less Quantity of Silver in a Crown-Piece, it will buy a less Quantity of Goods: Or if the Crown be rais'd to Six shillings, those Goods that us'd to be sold for a Crown will then cost Six shillings.
>
> That it will be the same in all Foreign Commodities and Foreign Exchange: For the Foreign Exchange and Par of money being only from an equal Quantity of Silver in the different Coins of the several Countries; if the money be made lighter, there must then be a greater number of pieces to make the Par, or Foreign Exchange by Foreign money equal, or else the Quantity of Silver will not be equal to

that in the Foreign Coin: So that the Foreign Exchange and Price of all Foreign Goods will rise in proportion to what the value of the money is rais'd. That which cost Twenty pounds before, will cost five and twenty if the money be raised a fifth; because there will be no greater a Quantity of Silver in Five and twenty pounds, than there was in Twenty before the money was raised.

That the raising the value of the money will not prevent the carrying it away, because that depends upon the Balance of Trade. For if there be more Foreign Goods bought of any Nation and Imported, than there are of the Native Commodities Exported, the Balance must be paid in money, which will always carry it out to pay the Debt till the Balance of that Nation be alter'd; which is, by Exporting more of the Native Commodities, and Importing less of the Foreign.

That there will be a great loss to all the Creditors and Landlords of England; for they letting their Land by the same rule which is by the Quantity of Silver in the money; if the money be made lighter by a fifth part, they will lose a fifth part by their Rent: They'll receive but Eighty pounds instead of an Hundred, because there will be no more Silver in an Hundred, than there was before in Eighty.

That there will be the same loss to the Creditors when they are paid their Bonds, Debts and Contracts; so that the raising of the money will put a very great Loss and Hardship upon Landlords and Creditors, and bring no advantage to the Nation.

The contrary Propositions in Answer to Mr. Lock are these:

That there is no Intrinsick Value in Silver, or any fixt or

certain Estimate that common consent hath placed on it; but that it is a Commodity, and riseth and falleth as other Commodities do.

That Money is the Instrument and Measure of Commerce, and not Silver.

That it is the Instrument of Commerce from the Authority of that Government where it is Coined; and that by the Stamp and Size of each piece the value is known.

That Money differs from Uncoined Silver in this, That the Authority of the Government gives a fixt and certain value to each piece of Money, which is generally beyond the value of the Silver in it.

That it is Money that men give, take and contract with for all other Commodities, and by which they estimate the value of all other things; having regard more to the stamp and currancy of the Money, than to the quantity of fine Silver in each piece.

That raising the Value of the Money, will not raise the Foreign Exchange, nor Foreign Commodities.

That if by the Balance of Trade in a Nation the Money is carried away, the only means to prevent it, is to raise the Value of the Money.

That it is the Practice of all the Governments in Europe, to raise their Money from time to time, as the price of Silver rises.

That the raising of the Money, will not raise the Value of any Commodities.

That if the Money be rais'd a fifth, the Landlord will not lose any part of his Rent, nor the Creditor any part of his Debt or Contract.

That if the Money be not rais'd, and kept above the price of Silver, it will be melted down, and carried away.

That the Consequence will be, That for want of Money, Commerce and Trade will be at a stand, the Price of the Native Commodities, and the Rents of the Lands will fall, and that it will cause a general Clamour and Poverty in the Nation.

To prove the Truth of these Propositions, it will be necessary to discourse in general of these several things, viz.

Of Riches, and the Value of Things.

Of Money, and the Par of the several Coins.

Of the Balance of Trade, and Foreign Exchange.

Of raising the Value of Money, with the Causes of it, and the Effects.

OF RICHES

AND

THE VALUE OF THINGS

All the Arguments in Mr. Lock's Book against the raising the Value of Money, are drawn from this single Supposition, That there is an Intrinsick Value in Silver, which is the Price or Estimate that Common Consent hath placed on it, by which it comes to be the Measure of the Value of all other Things: which, if that should not be true, then all his Consequences must be mistaken.

And to prove that he is so, It will be necessary to discourse of RICHES in general, and to shew how the Value of Things do arise.

By Riches, is meant all such Things as are of great Value.

By Value, is to be understood the Price of Things; that is, what any thing is worth to be sold: according to the old Maxim, Valet quantum vendi potest.

The Value of all Things, arise from their Use.

Things of no Use, are of no Value; as the English Phrase is, They are good for nothing.

There are two general Uses by which all Things have a Value: They are either useful to supply the Wants of the Body, or the Wants of the Mind.

Things that have a Value from being necessary to supply the Wants of the Body, are all such Things as are useful to support Life, such as all sorts of Food and Physick.

Things that have their Value by being useful to supply the Wants of the Mind, are all such Things that satisfy Desire, (Desire implies Want; it is the Appetite of the Mind, and as natural as Hunger to the Body:) such are all those Things that are any ways useful to satisfy the Mind, by contributing to the Ease, Pleasure, or Pomp of Life.

By supplying these two general Wants, all sorts of Things have a Value: But the greatest Number of them have their Value from supplying the Wants of the Mind; and Things of the greatest Value are used, to set orth the Pomp of Life; such as all sorts of fine Draperies, Gold; Silver, Pearl, Diamonds, and all sorts of precious Stones. They are used to adorn and deck the Body. They are Badges of Riches, and serve to make distinction of Preference amongst men.

These two general Wants Mankind is born with, and they are so natural to him, that he is better distinguished by what he wants, than what he enjoys. A Poor Man wants a Pound, a Rich Man an Hundred, others Thousands, and a Prince Hundreds of Thousands. Desire and Wants increase with Riches. And from thence it is, that the Contented Man is the only Rich Man, because he wants nothing.

Things that supply the Wants of the Body, and support Life, may be accounted to have a real and natural value: They are at all times and in all places of value; and if any things could have an Intrinsick Value in themselves, they would be Cattel and Corn; and therefore in Ancient times the computation of Riches was by the number of Cattel, according to the saying, *Pauperis est numerare pecus.*

Some are of an opinion, that there is a real Intrinsick value in Gold and Silver, and that they are only to be accounted Riches or Treasure.

This, it seems, has been an ancient opinion, which Ovid endeavours to confute by the Story of Midas. For Bacchus being entertained by Midas at a Feast, told him, in requital, he would give him whatsoever he should desire; and being of an opinion that Gold was the only Riches, desir'd that whatsoever he touch'd might be turn'd into Gold. His request was granted, with which he was very well pleased; but being hungry, was convinc'd of his Mistake: For as soon as he touch'd his Wine and Meat, they turn'd into Gold; and Midas had been starv'd, had not Bacchus for his kind entertainment sent him to a River to wash in, and gave him leave to change his Gold for Water, after he had experienc'd that Water was of more value to quench his thirst than Gold.

Things that supply the wants of the Mind, have only an Imaginary or Artificial Value, which depends only on opinion, and change their Values according to the Humor and Fancy of the persons that use them; and are like rich Apparel, that lose their Value because they are out of fashion.

It is the occasion and usefulness of things that creates the Value of them: And it is the Plenty or Scarcity of things, in respect of their occasion or use, that makes them of greater or lesser Value: Plenty makes things Cheap, and Scarcity Dear.

By this rule the Value of all things is governed; because the Value of things depending only on their use, if there be more than can be used, the remainder can be of no Use, and so of no Value. For the two common wants of the Body and Mind being either for Food or Ornament; those Commodities that are for

Food are perishable, and if not us'd in time, are lost and good for nothing; and those Commodities that are for Ornament, Plenty making them common and cheap, lose their use, and from thence their Value.

Rarity and Scarcity are the chief reasons for the value of those things that are us'd for Ornament, and not for any excellent quality in the things themselves. That's the reason that a Bracelet of Glass-Beads is of more value in Guiney than a Bracelet of Gold; because it is there more rare, those people being not acquainted with the Art of making Glass, and having more plenty of Gold than Glass; and by the same reason, Knives, and things made of Iron and Steel are of more value in those Countries where there are no Iron-Mines, and have plenty of Silver-Mines: And if the value of things were to arise from the Qualities that belong to them, those Things that are made of Iron and Steel, ought to have a greater Value than those that are made of Silver, because they are much more useful.

There is nothing that troubles this Controversy more, than for want of distinguishing betwixt Value and Vertue.

Value is only the Price of Things: That can never be certain, because it must be then at all times, and in all places, of the same Value; therefore nothing can have an Intrinsick Value.

But Things have an Intrinsick Vertue in themselves, which in all places have the same Vertue; as the Loadstone to attract Iron, and the several qualities that belong to Herbs, and Drugs, some Purgative, some Diuretical, &c. But these things, though they may have great Virtues, may be of small or no Value or Price, according to the place where they are plenty or scarce; as the Red-Nettle, though it be of excellent Virtue to stop Bleeding, yet here it is a Weed of no Value from its plenty: And so are Spices and Drugs in their own Native soil of no value, but as common Shrubs and Weeds; but with us of great Value, and yet in both places of the same Excellent Intrinsick Vertues.

Things common have no Value: For no Man will pay for that which he may have for gathering.

The Plenty of one Commodity do's not alter the Value of another, unless it be for the same use. Plenty of Iron or Lead will not make either Corn or Cloth cheaper or dearer, because Iron or Lead can neither supply the want of Food or Clothing.

Gold and Silver are Commodities as well as Lead or Iron; and according to their Plenty or Scarcity will make those things that are made of them Dearer or Cheaper; to wit, Gold and Silver-Plate, Lace, &c. but they cannot make Corn, Cloth, Lead, or Iron Dearer or Cheaper, because they cannot supply the uses of those Commodities.

There is no difference or distinction in things of equal Value: That is, one Commodity is as good as another that's of the same Value. An Hundred Pounds worth of Lead or Iron, is of as great a value as an Hundred Pounds worth of Silver or Gold: And an Hundred Pounds worth of course Cloth is of as great a value as an Hundred Pounds worth of fine. The Man is as Rich that has an Hundred Pounds worth of Corn or Cattel, as he that has an Hundred Pounds in Money by him, for his Corn and his Cattel may be soon turn'd into so much Money: And the Merchant and Trader are always changing their Money for Commodities, because they can get more by them than by Money; either by Transporting of them where such Commodities are most scarce, or else by changing the shapes of them, by which they are made more Useful, and thereby of more Value.

Now if the Value of all things arise from their use: If Plenty or Scarcity makes things Dear or Cheap: If Silver be a Commodity for several uses, and more plentiful in some places than in others; then it must necessarily follow, that Silver can have no Certain or Intrinsick Value, and if Silver be of an uncertain Value, then it can never be the Instrument of Commerce and Traffick: For, that which it uncertain in its own

Value, can never be a certain Measure of another Value.

Mr. Lock agrees this Consequence, and in Page 21 allows Gold, and Lead, and other Metals to be Commodities of uncertain values, and therefore cannot be the Measure of another value; but it do's not appear to me why he has separated Silver from Gold, which in all Discourses us'd to go together; or why that should not be a Commodity as well as other Metals, which, had he pleas'd to have allow'd, would have much shorten'd the Debate.

What Mr. Lock means when he says that the Intrinsick Value of Silver is the Estimate that common consent hath placed on it, I do not well understand, therefore must be excused if I do not well answer it. If he means that the Estimate that Common consent hath placed on Silver, that Mankind have agreed to set a certain and fixt Price upon Silver; he ought to have given account how and when they made such agreement; I must confess I never hear'd of any; if there was any such, it must be lately: For there is no Goldsmith that has been any considerable time at his Trade, but has bought the same Sterling Silver for Four Shillings Eight pence, Four and Ten pence, and Five Shillings per Ounce, for which he has given Five and Eight pence, Five and Ten pence, and Six shillings per Ounce.

If he means by the Estimate that Common consent hath placed on Silver, That all Governments have agreed to make their Silver Monies equal both for Weight and Fineness, that too will prove a mistake. For the Silver Coins in all Governments in Europe have been at one time or other raised and alter'd; and they never did agree in equal Quantities of fine Silver, as will be shown in the Discourse of Money, and the Par of the several Coins.

That which I have endeavour'd to prove in this Discourse, of Riches, and the Value of Things, are these Five several Maxims, which I have here set together, because I shall have occasion to make use of them hereafter. viz.

1. That nothing has a Price or Value in it self.

2. That the Price or Value of every thing arises from the occasion or use for it.

3. That Plenty and Scarcity, in respect to their occasion, makes things of greater or lesser Value.

4. That the Plenty or Scarcity of one Commodity do's not alter the Prices of other Commodities which are not for the same uses.

5. That in Trade and Commerce there is no difference in Commodities when their Values are equal; that is, Twenty shillings worth of Lead or Iron to some Merchants is the same as Twenty shillings in Silver or Gold.

OF MONEY,

AND

THE PAR OF THE SEVERAL COINS.

MR. Lock says, pag: 22. That Money differs from Uncoin'd Silver only in this, That the Quantity of Silver in each piece of Money, is ascertain'd by the Stamp it bears; which is set there, to be a Publick Voucher of its Weight and Fineness.

That it is the Quantity of Silver Mankind give or take, or contract for, that they estimate the value of other things, and satisfy for them; and thus by its Quantity, Silver becomes the Measure of Commerce.

The Question betwixt us here will be, Whether Money has its sole Value from the Quantity of Silver in each piece of Coin? Or whether Money has not some Value from the Authority of the Government where it is Coin'd, above the Value of the Silver in each piece?

For the better answering this Question, it will be necessary to discourse in general of Money, and the Par of the several Coins.

Money is a Value given to a piece of Metal by the Stamp of Publick Authority, which is commonly greater than the Value of the Metal that bears the Impression.

The Value of each piece of Money is known by the difference of the Stamp, Size and Colour of the piece.

Money is commonly made of some Metal, but it is more for conveniency, than of absolute necessity. For the Value arising from Publick Authority, it may as well be set to any thing else that is as convenient, and can be as well preserv'd from being counterfeited. For in several Countries Money is not made of Metals; as in some parts of Guiney Money is made of Shells. And Mr. Lock observes, in India Money is by Yards of Wampompeak. And in England it was formerly made of Leather, and from thence came the Name of a Hide of Land, which did as well describe the value of Land, now to say ten, twenty, or a hundred pounds worth of Land.

In ancient times, in the most civiliz'd parts of the world, the Money was made of Copper or Brass.

It was Four hundred eighty four years before the Romans had any Silver Money, and Sixty two years after, before they had any Money made of Gold. And had but very little of either, till they had greatly enlarg'd their Empire. And from the Spoils of those conquer'd rich Cities, Carthage, Athens, and Alexandria, brought a greater plenty of Silver and Gold into their Exchequer. And it always continued scarce in Europe, till the discovery of the West-Indies.

There are now in most Countries of Europe three sorts of Money, Copper, Gold, and Silver Money, and they are of equal Value, according to what they are stamp'd at. The Farthings of England, the Duyts of Holland, the Deniers of France, the Reas of Portugal, and the Malvedies of Spain, &c. do buy and pay for all sorts of Commodities, as well as the Money that is made of Silver or Gold. And the Merchants both in their Bills of Exchange, and in their Accompts, do as often reckon by the Copper Money, as by the Silver Money. And the Computation of the Silver Money is often made from the Value of the Copper Money; as in Portugal, the Merchant does often draw his Bills of Exchange to be paid in Rials of Four hundred Reas, or Four hundred and fifty Reas.

And so in Spain, he draws his Bill to be paid in Rials of Three hundred seventy two Malvedies, or more, according to the rise of the Exchange. And in Holland some Merchants draw their Bills to be paid by Groats, which is a base Money, as well as others do to be paid by Shillings.

For the Value of Money arising from the Authority of the Government, if the Authority be the same, the Value of the Copper, Silver, or Gold money, must be the same in proportion to what they are set at: And Copper being a Metal of lesser Value than either Gold or Silver, is much better to make small money of, because the pieces are thereby made larger and fitter for use and handling.

There are more Bargains made with Copper Money then either with Silver or Gold: For those Commodities that are bought in great parcels are sold by retail in small parcels for common use; and for one Bargain made with Silver or Gold Money, there are ten made with Copper Money. Five or Ten Quarter of Wheat which may cost Five or Ten Pound in Silver Money at one Bargain, is divided into Twopeny, Peny, and Halfpeny Loaves, and afterwards bought perhaps by a Hundred persons, and paid for by the Copper Money of the Countrey: And there are but few Bargains that can be made without the use of some Copper Money to make the Sum even. All Sums here in England between Sixpence and Twelvepence are made up with Farthings and Halfpence.

This shews Mr. Lock's mistake, where he says, That 'tis by the Quantity of Silver men give or take, or contract for, that they Estimate the Value of other things, and satisfy for them, &c.

For the Baker, the Grocer, the Coffee-man, and all the Retailers, sell great quantities of Goods for the Copper Money wherein there is not one grain of Silver, and yet they are as well paid and satisfied for their Goods with such Money, as the Farmer or Merchant of whom they first bought those Goods are with the Silver Money. For the Copper Money may be Coin'd as near to the Value of the Copper, as the Silver or Gold Money may be to the Value of the Silver or Gold; and the Authority of the Government that makes them all current being the same, all sorts of Money must be of an equal Value according to what they are Stamp'd at.

For the nature of the Metals can make no difference if the Values be equal: That being done only by proportioning the quantities of the Metals in each piece of Money to their different Values: For instance, supposing Copper to be at Twelvepence a pound, and Silver to be at Three pound per pound, an Ounce of Silver, which is Five Shillings, is equal to Five pound of Copper: And there being Threescore pence in Five Shillings, and Threescore Ounces in Five pound, an Ounce of Copper being a piece of money about the bigness of a Crown in Silver, is equal to the value of a Penny in Silver; and an Half-penny being half an Ounce, and of the size of Half-a-crown, is equal to an Half-penny in Silver.

If it had been the Quantity of Silver that Men take, and contract for, Men would have made their Bargains by the weight of Silver, and not by the tale of money: For Silver is as well divided for Traffick by weight, as money is divided by number, and there would be no occasion for Coining. For it is as easy in making of a Bargain, when the Question is ask'd, What shall I give? or what will you take for such and such Commodities? to say, I will give or take so many Grains, Penny-weight, Ounces, or Pounds of Silver; as to say, that I'll give or take so many Pounds, Shillings, Pence, or Half-pence.

But Silver being a Commodity for other Uses besides the making of money, and according to the Plenty or, Scarcity to supply those Occasions is dearer or cheaper; therefore money was invented, which by Publick Authority sets and fixeth a certain value to each piece of money; and it is that which men give and take by tale and number of the pieces, in exchange for all other Commodities, without regarding the weight and quantity of Silver in each piece. And if a man should offer to buy Goods in the Market, by saying, I'll give so many Grains, Ounces, or Pounds of Silver; he would be presently ask'd, What is Silver worth an Ounce? and would be no more understood by Mr. Lock's answer, That an Ounce of Silver is worth an Ounce of Silver, than if a Country-man in a market being ask'd, What is Corn worth a Bushel? should say, 'Tis worth a Bushel of Corn.

And yet if Mr. Lock's definition of money be true, That it differs from uncoin'd Silver only in this, That the Quantity of Silver in each piece of money, is ascertain'd by the Stamp it bears, which is set there to be a Publick Voucher of its weight and fineness; there can be no other Answer given to know the value of Silver by. For if the Stamp to a Crown-piece, which is an Ounce of Silver, be set only to describe its weight and fineness; if any man be ask'd the Question, What Silver is worth? he can mean no more when he says, 'Tis worth a Crown an Ounce, than that an Ounce of Silver is worth an Ounce of Silver: so that by his description of money, no man can describe the value of Silver.

But that Mr. Lock is mistaken in his definition of money, will appear more plainly, by discoursing of the Par of the several Coins.

He says, That the Par of Monies is certain number of pieces

of the Coin of one Country, containing an equal Quantity of Silver in another number of pieces of the Coin of another Country.

This is a general Opinion, and therefore it is no wonder to find it here asserted by a Gentleman who, I suppose is only acquainted with the Speculation and Theory of Foreign Coins; when many Merchants and Traders, whose business it has been to know the practick part, and the difference of the value of the several Coins, are of the same Opinion.

And yet if it be but consider'd, it will be found to be a vulgar Error; and that the Par of money is made, by computing the Valuation that the several Governments set on their Coins; which is not from the equal Quantity of Silver in each piece of money. For there is scarce two Mints that agree in the Standards of their Coin. The Standard of Spain is Eleven Ounces Four-penny weight fine, in a Pound Troy. Mexico Eleven Ounces Three-penny weight, Ten Grains. England Eleven Ounces Two-penny weight. France Ten Ounces Ten-penny weight. Holland Nine Ounces. And the same difference might be observ'd in all the other Mints of Europe.

Besides, The Pound Troy is divided into a number of pieces differing in their weight, and that no two Mints divide their money alike. That in most pieces of money the very Grains of Silver are divided, in some a tenth, thirteenth, fifteenth, twentieth part of a Grain and more; and that there is scarce any one piece of money without Fractions of Grains of Silver: so that in those very Coins that are nearest in value by computation, it will be found altogether impracticable for any Merchant to keep an account of the Par of the several Coins, by the quantity of Silver in each piece of money.

It would puzzle a good Arithmetician to state the difference of the Grains of Silver in those pieces that seem most to agree; as to Instance:

It is no easy matter to number the difference of Grains betwixt those Pieces of Eight, that of Mexico and Spain, with the Pound Troy, being both divided into thirteen pieces and an half.

It is much more difficult to examine the difference of the grains of silver in such pieces, as the Sixpence of England, the Riall of Spain, the Shilling of Holland, with other Coins about that value. But if the difference of the Grains, with the innumerable Fractions of Grains be examin'd in the Stivers of the Low-Countries, the Souz of France, the Crutizes of Germany, with the Silver Pence of England, and the rest of the small Silver monies of other Countries, it will be found almost impossible for the Merchant or any one else to keep an account of the quantity of Silver in each piece of Coin.

This difference in the Standards of the several Mints, and in the unequal division of their money, shews plainly that there is no common agreement about the quantity of Silver in their Coins, and that Mr. Lock is mistaken if this be his meaning of the Intrinsick Value of Silver, by the Estimate which common consent hath placed on it, by the quantity of Silver in their Coins.

If the measure of Commerce and Traffick were by the Quantity of Silver in the Coin, the Governments would certainly have agreed to have made their money of fine Silver without any Allay, and to have divided it into pieces of equal weight; or, if it had been necessary, to have put in some Allay, that the money might bear the impression the better, which is the Reason that Mr. Lock gives for doing it; all the Mints by this time would have certainly found out and agreed in that proportion which is most convenient for that purpose, or at least the greatest number of them. And therefore I cannot agree to his Reason for putting in an Allay; and the rather, because I have seen some Medals made of fine Silver that have bore the impression very well, and look'd more beautiful than the Stamp of any New-coin'd money. And anciently in England, from Osbright the Saxon King, to Edward III. the money was without any Allay. And the Coin of the Great Mogul is now made of all fine Silver, and bears the Stamp very well.

Besides, It seems to be the only Reason for making the money of such different Allays, that the quantity of Silver in each piece, and the mystery of the Mint, might not be easily discovered, and the money not be valued after the price of Bullion, and thereby prevent the Merchants, and those that deal in Bullion, from buying and selling the Coin, and melting it down upon a sudden rise of Bullion. And this might reasonably be thought a way to prevent it, because the knowledge of the different Allays and fineness of Gold and Silver, is a mystery that belongs only to a small number of men that deal in it; who are either Moniers that belong to Mints, or Goldsmiths that serve an Apprenticeship to acquire skill in it; and yet, perhaps, not all of those acquainted with the Chymical part of the mystery the knowledge of refining and essaying of Silver and Gold; but content themselves to judge of the difference of the fineness of the several Coins by the Touchstone, and colour of the Metal.

And it will yet more plainly appear, That men do not buy and sell by the quantity of Silver in the Coin, if it be consider'd, that the Merchants and Traders buy and sell all their Commodities by weight or measure, and often make their Contracts by the price of what one Yard, or one Pound will amount to; which price is generally for an odd sum of money, as Two-pence-farthing, Three-pence-farthing, Half-penny Three Farthings, &c. And that the loss of a Farthing in the Pound or Yard by the Par of the money, if they were to buy or sell by the quantity of Silver, would make a great alteration in the profit of the Bargain in a great sum, and much greater in the making of many Bargains, and a continued Trade; since it appears that there is no money without fractions in the grains of Silver.

Besides, It is no advantage to a Merchant to make a computation of the quantity of Silver in the several Foreign Coins: For he always makes up the Accompt of the Profit or Loss, by the mony of the Country where he lives; and there can be no Accompt made up, till the effects of his Commodities, which he sends out, are return'd. And if his Goods are sold by money not of the same Par to the Coin of his own Country, yet if such money buys the same quantity of Goods as the Coin of his own Country would do, it will be the same thing to him as if the money was Par, and that there was an equal quantity of Silver in the money that bought those Goods. For Instance: If an English Merchant sends into Portugal so many Serges, or other Commodities, as cost him here an hundred pounds, and they should be sold for the Reas, which is the Copper money of that Country, or other Coin of unequal Par; and with that money Portugal Wines are bought, and sent over into England: The Merchant makes up the Accompt when the Wines are sold, and if they produce him an hundred and twenty pounds clear of all charge, he gets twenty pound by the return. And 'tis to no purpose for him to take an Accompt of the difference of the Par betwixt the Portugal and English Coin, or whether his Goods were sold for Copper or Silver money.

If the Par of monies was to be reckon'd by the Quantity of Silver in each piece, and that men made their Bargains only for the quantity of Silver, to what purpose is there any Copper money coin'd? which, reckoning one Country with another, is a third part of all the money in Europe.

It's true, Mr. Lock will not allow any other but Silver money to be the measure of Commerce and Traffick; and refuseth Gold and all other Metals, because he allows them to be Commodities which rise and fall in their Value, and therefore not fit to make Money of. This is grounded upon the supposition, that there is an Intrinsick Value in Silver, and therefore do's not alter its Price. As to the Intrinsick I have already answer'd; and as to that, whether Gold and Copper are not as fit to make Money of as Silver, I'll leave it to those that continually take them in Payments, to give a reason why they take such Money, if they did not think the Value of them to be as good as the Silver Money.

Money at all times, and in all places, has been made of Copper and Gold: And if they should not be allow'd as Money, there would not be enough left to carry on Commerce and Traffick.

'Tis the Publick Authority upon the Metal that makes it Money; and without such Authority, Silver would no more pass for Money than Gold. There can't be a plainer demonstration of this, than by what appears since the Parliament has been debating about New Coining of the Money, and setling the Value of the Guineas: For, before their meeting, the Clipt Money pass'd currant, as if it were Unclipt. But their Considerations about calling of it in, presently put a stop to the currancy of it; because, by their Debates, the Value of it was made uncertain, and no man knew where the Loss would fall. And the same may be observ'd from their Debates about setling the price of Guineas; For Guineas, before their meeting, went currant at Thirty shilings; but, upon the House of Commons voting that they should not exceed Eight and twenty, every man presently refus'd to take 'em for more. And upon another resolution, That they should not exceed Six and twenty, and not declaring at what price they should be currant, no man since will take them for more than Six and twenty, most refuse to take 'em at so much, and some refuse the taking of 'em at any price: So that Silver would no more pass for Money than Gold, unless the price of each piece were fixt by Publick Authority.

The Argument that has been us'd to shew that 'tis impracticable to make up the Par of the Coins from the quantity of Money in each piece, because of the great difference in the Standard; the unequal division of the Money, and the Infinite number of fractions in the quantity of Silver in every piece, is of use to prove that the Par of Monies is from the Valuation that each Government sets up on their Coin: Or else there could be no Bargain made upon an equal foot, there being such a certain difference in the Quantity of the Silver in the several Coins, which could never be remedied unless publick Authority had fixt the Value to their Money, by which all those Fractions and Inequalities in the several Coins are even'd. And one piece of Money is as good as another in the Countrey where each piece is Coin'd according to the Valuation that is set upon it, which is describ'd by the Stamp and Size of the piece, tho' they differ greatly in the Quantity of Silver.

Now if it be true in it self, That nothing has a Value or Price: That the Value of all things arises from their Use, it will be no strange Consequence that Money should have a Value, from the great use of it, above the price of Bullion, or the Metal that bears the Impression: And that the Government should have power to set and fix a Value or Price upon their Money, as well as the Merchant and Trader upon their Goods and Wares: And that 'tis as reasonable to allow the Government some Value for their Stamp upon their Money above the price of the Metal, as to pay the Goldsmiths for the Fashion of their Plate,or the Ingraver or Carver for the Impression on his Medal. And why should it seem so strange that a new piece of Coin should have a Value above the price of the Metal, which is seldom above Sixpence or Eight pence in Five shillings, being not above a Tenth part more than the Value of the Metal, when an old piece of Coin grown scarce, is seldom less than double the Value; and some of them exceed ten, twenty, and a hundred times the

Value of the Metal. A Mill'd Crown of Oliver's is now worth Twenty shillings to be sold; and an Otho's Head, and some other Roman Coins, are worth a hundred times the Value of the Metal that bears the Impression.

Besides, there is a greater reason for the Value of the Money; because by the Authority of the Government it is made current and lawful Money, and every body is oblig'd to take it; and therefore no person can be a loser by taking of it, because another person is to take it of him again for the same Value.

The Stamp upon the Money is the Seal of the Government; so that if there was nota Law to make it current, and had only the King's Seal or Stamp upon it, it ought rather to have a better, or at least the same Value as a Bank Note, or any Private Person's Bond or Seal; which only shews, that the person whose Note or Seal it is, is oblig'd to pay or exchange it. And it there were no other obligation from the King's Stamp than to show that the King would take it in his Revenue, it would give it a sufficient currency, tho' there were no Law to make it current.

It is the currancy of the Coin that all men regard more than the quantity of the Siver init: For the difference of the Fineness of the Silver, and the number of the grains in each piece of Silver, few persons are acquainted with. Not one in a thousand can tell how many grains of fine Silver there are in a Crown, Halfcrown, Shilling, or Sixpence. Therefore, to what purpose should the Stamp be set to be a Voucher to the Weight and Fineness, as Mr. Locke affirms, which no person inquires after or desires to know. 'Tis the Currant and Lawful Money of England that men contract for, and oblige themselves in their Bonds to pay; and if it were the quantity of Silver in the Money that men regarded, they certainly would express it in their Bonds and Contracts; and have said Currant and Lawful Money containing so many Ounces and Grains of fine Silver. For, Money do's wear and grow lighter by often telling over; so that if it were true, that 'tis the quantity of Silver in the Money that men give, take, and contract for in exchange for all other Commodities, they ought to make their Bargains to be paid in Money Coin'd such and such a year, and so set the Price of their Goods according to the Date of the year the Money was Coin'd in: Or else they will lose more by the difference in the quantity of Silver, by the age and wearing of the Money, than the profit by the Goods amounts to. For 'tis very plain, that the old Unclipp'd Broad Money of England is worn Ten per Cent. lighter than the new-Mill'd Money: So that is the quantity of the Silver in the Money were to be regarded, it would make Ten per Cent. difference in the profit of the Bargain. And yet no man will deny, but that the Broad Unclipp'd Money will buy as many Goods of the same Value, as the New-mill'd Money will do: And that all Bonds and Contracts are as well paid and satisfied by such old Money, as by the new.

It is the Denomination and Currency of the Money that men regard in Bargaining, and not the quantity of Silver: For in all parts of Europe men buy and sell by the Denomination of several sorts of Money, both of Gold and Silver, that were formerly currant, but now out of Use, and not in being: As by several sorts of Dollars, Guilder-Pieces, Florens, Marks, Nobles, and Groats of England, &c. For when Princes are forced by the rise of Bullion to raise their Coin and make their Money lighter, they often change the Denomination; and yet men keep their custom of making their Bargains by the old Weighty Money, and pay for their Goods by the New-coin'd lighter Money. As to instance; in many Countries here in England, they buy and sell their Cattel by Groats and Nobles, which was the currant Money, and way of reckoning till Edward the VIth's days; there being till then, very little other Silver Money Coin'd but Groats, and they were double the weight in proportion to what the Money is now Coin'd at. And yet in paying and receiving they expect no more than to be paid by the now current Money, though the quantity of Silver be much less in this Money.

The Judges in setting their Fines commonly use the old Denomination of a Mark, which is the name of the Weight of Gold and Silver in most places of Europe, contains Eight Ounces of the pound Troy; and in Edward the Third's time, when our pound Sterling weigh'd a pound Troy, a Mark was a common name in payment, which then contain'd Eight Ounces of Silver; and yet the Judges by their Fine, intend no more than that it should be paid by the Current Money now in being, which is two Thirds of a pound Sterling by tale, and not two Thirds of a pound Troy by Weight, as the Mark signifi'd when first in Use, which would now amount to Forty shillings by Tale, instead of Thirteen and Four pence; which shews that Money is paid by a computed Valuation, and not by the quantity of Silver in it.

The same may be observ'd in examining the Par of the several Coins; and that the Par of Money is made solely by the Valuation of the Coin according to what it is current at, and not from the quantity of Silver in each piece. In the Reign of Queen Elizabeth, Anno 1586. there was a Par of Monies agreed on betwixt the Earl of Essex, and the States of the United Provinces; which was, That Three and thirty of their shillings and Four Stivers, should be equal to our Twenty shillings, an English shilling being then valu'd at 10 Stivers. And if any person will examine the quantity of Silver in this Par, they will find that there is more Silver in our Twenty shillings, than in Eight and Thirty shillings of their Money. In the year 1622, the States set out a Placate, wherein they prohibited all Foreign Coins to pass, except what were nam'd in that Ordinance of the States, according to the Valuation there express'd, The English shillings was one of the Foreign Coins that was allow'd to be there current, which was to pass for Ten Stivers and an half;

so that by this second Valuation of our English Money, they allow'd the Par of our Twenty shillings, to be equal to Five and Thirty shillings two Stivers of their Money; and yet our shilling was made lighter betwixt the first time of the Valuation and the second, by Two shillings in Three pounds. The French Crown, which us'd to pass for Five and fifty Stivers, is now current in Flanders for Seven and fifty Stivers, since the French have rais'd the Value of their Money; though there is no more Silver in the Crown-piece than there was before; which shews plainly that the Par of Monies is a computed Valuation, and not from the quantity of Silver in each piece of Coin.

There is a Par betwixt the Monies made of Gold and Silver: That likewise is uncertain, and depends somewhat upon the Valuation of the Money; but because Gold is a Commodity of great Value, the Gold Money is generally Coin'd nearer to the Market-price of Gold, than the Silver Money is to the Silver; and therefore the Gold Money is often weigh'd, because the difference of a grain or two greatly alters the Value of the Piece of Money.

To shew what the Par is betwixt Gold and Silver, will be more proper in the Discourse of raising the Coin; therefore I shall conclude this Debate of money, and the Par of money, and submit the Question betwixt us to consideration upon the Arguments that have been us'd to prove, That Money has some Valuation from the Authority of the Government where 'tis Coin'd, and not its sole Value from the quantity of Silver in each piece.

That men regard the Currency and Stamp of the Coin, and take it more upon the account that it will pass again for the same value to another, than for the quantity of Silver in each piece.

And not as Mr. Lock has asserted; that is,

That the Stamp upon the Money is set there only to be a

Publick Voucher of its weight and fineness.

That in buying and selling, ‘tis the quantity of Silver that men give or take, or contract for, that they estimate the value of other things, and satisfy for them; and thus by its quantity, Silver becomes the measure of Commerce.

OF THE BALANCE OF TRADE,

AND

FOREIGN EXCHANGE.

The Balance of Trade, is us'd by Mr.Lock as an Argument against raising the Value of the Money; because the Balance of all Foreign Accompts, as he supposes, are paid in Money, which must be sent out to balance the Accompt; and let the Value of it be what it will that is set upon the Money, it will go for no more in Foreign Countries, than according to the quantity of Silver that is in it.

This is a very popular Notion, and generally believ'd; yet if it be consider'd, it will be found to be a mistake, and that there is no such Usage as Balancing the Foreign Accompts of Merchants, by the Money of a Foreign Nation: But, if there were such an Usage, 'tis the greatest Argument for raising the Value of the Money.

That which is commonly meant by the Balance of Trade, is the equal importing of Foreign Commodities, with the exporting of the Native. And they reckon that Nation has the advantage in the Balance of Trade, that exports more of the

Native Commodities, and imports less of the Foreign. And the reason that is given for it is, That if the Native Commodities be of a greater Value that are exported, the Balance of that Accompt must be made up in Bullion or Money; and the Nation grows so much richer, as the Balance of that Account amounts to.

This Opinion is grounded upon this Supposition, That Gold and Silver are the only Riches.

Some men lay so great a stress about the enquiring into this Balance, that they are of Opinion, That a Trading Nation may be ruin'd and undone, if there been't Care taken, by Laws, to regulate the Balance. And yet there is nothing so difficult, as to find out the Balance of Trade in any Nation; or to know whether there ever was, or can be such a thing as the making up the Balance of Trade betwixt one Nation and another; or to prove, if it could be found out, that there is any thing got or lost by the Balance.

For a Nation, as a Nation, never Trades; 'tis only the Inhabitants and Subjects of each Nation that Trade: And there are no set days or times for making up of a general Accompt, every Merchant makes up his own private Accompt; and that's not done at any set time, one Merchant makes it up one week, and another in another week; so that there can be no set time when to begin that Balance.

Therefore those that rely so much upon finding out the Balance of Trade, do it by taking the Computation from the Trade of several years of one Nation with another, and think it may be done by examining the Accompt of the Custom-House Books, and us'd to give for Instance the French Trade; because the Revenue that arose from those Duties on French Wines, and other Commodities that were imported, were so much greater than the Duties on those Goods that were sent into France, and therefore us'd to cry out very much against the

French Trade: Tho', perhaps, if that were throughly consider'd, the French Trade was as profitable to the Nation as any other Foreign Trade; which might be made to appear, if it were proper for this Debate.

But to make up the Balance of Trade by the Custom-House Books, is a very uncertain way of reckoning: For all Foreign Goods that are imported, pay a greater Duty than the Native Goods exported. 'Tis the Interest of all Trading Nations to lay easy Customs (if any) upon their Native Commodities, that they may be sent cheap to Foreign Markets, and thereby encourage both the making and exporting of them: And to lay high Duties upon Foreign Wares, that they might be dear, and so not lessen by their cheapness the consumption of the Native Commodities: So that there can be no Computation of the Balance of Trade from the difference of the Sum of Money that's paid at the Custom-House for the Foreign Goods imported, and the Native exported.

But suppose there should be an Allowance made, in casting up the Accompt, for the greatness of the Duties that the Foreign Goods pay more than the Native, yet that can be no advantage in the discovering the Balance of Trade; because they cannot discover by the Custom-House Books, what the Native Goods that are exported are sold for: For the Balance of the Trade must arise from the Value of the Goods that are sold, and not from the Quantity that are exported or imported. And that's known only to the Merchant that sells the Goods, and 'tis not for his Interest to acquaint others with it, and thereby discover the Profits of his Trade: So that there can be no finding out the Balance of Trade by the Custom-House Books.

Some are of the opinion, that the way to find out the Balance of Trade, is by the Foreign Exchange. And they reckon that if the Exchange run high upon a Nation, 'tis a sign that there are more Foreign Goods imported, than there are of the Native exported; and therefore there are Bills of Exchange drawn to answer the Effects, and make up the difference in the Value of what the Native Goods were sold for less than the Foreign. This seems to be the nearest way of guessing of the Balance of the Trade of a Nation; but this is altogether as uncertain.

For Exchanges rise and fall every week, and at some particular times in the year run high against a Nation, and at other times run as high on the contrary. As against a Vintage, a great Mart, or some Publick Sale, the Exchange may run higher to Bourdeaux, Francfort, or Holland, upon an East-India Sale: And at other times the Exchange may have run to the same places as much on the contrary; for no Exchange can constantly run high against a Nation; for then the Merchants that trade to that Country, must always lose by their Trade: For if the Goods that they export, don't yield them as much profit as the Goods they import, they must lose by the Return. And it cannot be suppos'd that Merchants will always Trade to a Country, where they must always lose by Trading; therefore there can be no account of the Balance of Trade by Foreign Exchange.

As to the rise of the Exchange betwixt Holland and England, that's not to be reckon'd as a Rule, because of the extraordinary charge of the War at this time.

But if there could be an account taken of the Balance of Trade, I can't see where the advantage of it could be. For the reason that's given for it, That the Overplus is paid in Bullion, and the Nation grows so much the richer, because the Balance is made up in Bullion, is altogether a mistake: For Gold and Silver are but Commodities; and one sort of Commodity is as good as another, so it be of the same value. An hundred pounds worth of Copper is as good to a Merchant, as if he imported an hundred pounds worth of Silver, and he may get as much by it. Besides, some Countries have no Gold and Silver, and yet the Trade to these Countries may be as profitable to the Merchant and Nation, as to the other Countries from whence they fetch the Gold and Silver; as the Trade to Denmark and Sueden, and the Northern parts of the World, from whence they fetch Pitch, Tar, Hemp, and Timber, is as profitable to England, as the Trade to Spain, from whence the Merchant fetches the Bullion; tho' those very Goods, Pitch, Tar, Hemp, &c. are bought, for the most part, with the Bullion that's brought from Spain: For all Merchants get by their Trade; and if they grow rich, the Nation thrives.

For a Nation grows rich, by the Inhabitants growing rich. Besides, those Goods, Pitch, Tar, and Hemp, are more profitable Commodities to England, than Bullion; because they are Materials for the building of Ships, and employ more hands in the working of them after they are imported, than Bullion does.

And the only way to know what sort of Goods and Trade are most profitable to a Nation, is by examining which sort of Goods employ most hands by importing and manufacturing. For every man that works, is paid for his time; and the more there are employ'd in a Nation, the richer the Nation grows: And therefore the importing of unwrought Goods, such as Flax, Raw-silk, Cottons, &c. and all sorts of bulky and weighty Goods, such as Wine, Pitch, Tar, &c. are more profitable to a Nation, than Wrought-silks, Linnens or Callicoes; or Gold, Silver, and Goods of little Bulk in respect to their weight: Because the Nation gets the profit by the making of the Raw silk, Flax and Cottons into Wrought silks, Linnen, and all such things as are made of of Cotton. And by the bulky Goods, a great profit from their Freight. But this Rule all Trading Nations are acquainted with, and therefore lay high Duties upon all manufactur'd Goods, and a less Duty upon those unmanufactur'd.

Some, upon this Consideration, are for prohibiting not

only almost all sorts of manufactur'd Goods, but several other Commodities; because they think they hinder the making and consuming of their own Manufactures, and Native Commodities. But in this they are under a great mistake; and, perhaps, there is nothing so prejudicial to the Trade of England, as the many Laws for prohibiting Commodities, or laying too high a Duty, which amounts to a Prohibition: For by such Prohibition, the Trade to such a Country is wholly lost, by which the profit that the English Merchant us'd to get by selling the Foreign Goods, the profit of the Owners of the Ship for the Freight, the profit from the Native Commodities that us'd to be sent in Exchange, with the profit of the Customs to the Government, are lost. By such Laws, several sorts of Linnens, and other Commodities, are prohibited, and the Trade to several parts of Germany, Russia, Muscovy, &c. is thereby almost lost.

A well-regulated and proportion'd Duty laid upon Foreign Wares, may be very useful to a Trading Nation; but then it must be so proportion'd, that it may not hinder the importation of such Foreign Goods, nor lessen the make and consumption of the Native Commodities that are for the same uses; which may be done by setting the Duties so high, as that the Native Commodities maybe afforded much cheaper. And then the Foreign Wares will only be bought and us'd by the richer sort of People, and the Native Commodities will be us'd by the rest, which are the great Body of the People, that cause the great consumption. And that proportion of the Native Commodities which, perhaps, might have been us'd by the richer sort, if such Foreign Wares had not been imported, will be exported in Exchange by the Merchant, and be consum'd by the richer People of those Countries from whence such Goods were imported: So that the same quantity of the Native Commodities will be made and consum'd; the Owners of Ships, and Mariners, will have profit by the Freight; the Merchant by his Trade, and the King by his Customs.

For things have no Value in themselves; It is opinion and fashion brings them into use, and gives them a value: And all Foreign Wares, especially the dearer sort, are us'd chiefly for Ornaments, and as Badges of Riches, because they are Foreign and rare; and not from any extraordinary quality or goodness in the make of them. And the same humor and opinion is in all Nations. The French value the English Cloth, Hats, Gloves, and other English Wares, more than their own; as we us'd to do French Stuffs, Hats, and Jessamin Gloves, and other French Goods. And this particular humor and opinion of valuing Foreign Commodities, is the chief support of Foreign Trade, which is so beneficial to all Nations. Therefore there is nothing of so great a Concern to a Trading Nation, as the well-regulating the Custom House Rates.

Those Gentlemen that discourse much of the Balance of Trade, do often find fault with the wearing and consuming so much Foreign Wares, which hinder, in their opinion, the consumption of the Native. And therefore us'd to exclaim much against the wearing of Silk, and drinking so much French, and other Wines: And do believe, that if such quantities of Foreign Goods were not imported and worn, the Return would be made in Bullion, which would make the Nation much richer. This is their general Complaint: But, if it be consider'd, it will be found that there is little reason for't; and that the wearing of Silk, may be as profitable to the Nation as the wearing of Cloth. That the importing of Wines makes the Nation as rich, as by importing of Bullion. And that if the Inhabitants did not wear Silk, and drink Wine, they would neither have Silk, Wine, nor Bullion.

For this is a certain Maxim in Trade, That the foundation of all Foreign Trade is from the Native or Staple Commodities of each Country. It is by the Exchange of the Staple Commodities of England, Tin, Lead, and all sorts of Woollen Manufactures, that Gold, Silver, Silk, Wines, and all sorts of Foreign Goods are imported. And as a Nation has nothing else at first to begin Traffick, but with its Native Commodities, so it cannot be continued without. And whensoever those are prohibited, the Trade to that Country must be lost, with the profit that was got by that Trade;) for there is no Foreign Trade but is profitable to a Nation, or at least may be made so;) and it is not for the Interest of a Trading Nation, to use none but their own Native Commodities. And therefore if Silks were not worn here, then there would be none imported; nor no Cloth nor Serges exported and worn in those Countries from whence we fetch our Silk: because they have nothing to give in Exchange but Silk, which is their Native Commodity.

And it is more profitable for the Nation, that the Woollen Manufactures should be worn in Foreign Countries, than in their own: because the profit of the carriage, which is the exporting of the Woollen Manufactures, and importing of the Silk, is gain'd by it. And the same general Rule maybe observ'd in the Trade for Wines, and all Foreign Wares.

And tho' the importing of Wines be extremely cry'd out against, yet it is one of the best Trades to England; for, being a very bulky Commodity, it pays a great Freight: And being for the use of the richer People, it pays a greater Duty to the King, and that without complaint. For England being an Island, and the Riches and Strength of it being from Trade and Shipping, those Commodities that are bulky, ought to be valued as most profitable.

And if some Gentlemen object, That the greatest part of the French Wines us'd to be bought with Bullion: They will answer themselves, if they reflect that we have no Bullion here in England; and therefore must have it at first by the Exchange of some of our Native Commodities. And if it be fetch'd from Spain by Bays, Serges, or other Commodities, and afterwards carried into France, that's no disadvantage: For the Merchants are paid for the double carriage of it, in the price of the Wines by those that sell 'em; for every Merchant expects profit in making his Bargain.

But some Gentlemen are of opinion, That it is a great disadvantage to a Nation to carry out the Bullion, which is a Treasure, and not perishable; and bring in Wines that are consum'd, and the Nation never the richer for them after they are drank. And it is by this way that they make up the account of the Balance, whether a Nation gets or loses by Trade, And for Argument, commonly use a Simile, formerly publish'd by Mr. Mun in his Discourse of the Balance of Trade; and compare the Stock of a Nation to a private person, suppos'd to have a thousand pound a year, and two thousand pound in his Chest: If he spends fifteen hundred a year, in four years time his two thousand pound will be spent. And so on the contrary, if he spends but five hundred pounds a year, in the same time he will double his money in his Chest. The same will be to a Nation; so much as is imported and consumed more of the Foreign Commodities than is exported of the Native, so much will the Stock of the Nation be wasted. And so on the contrary, by how much less is consumed of Foreign Wares than is exported of the Native, so much will the Stock of the Nation be increased, because the Balance on either side must be return'd in Bullion.

Upon this Simile is founded the opinion for the Balance of Trade, which is to enquire, Whether a Nation gets or loses by any particular Trade, from the difference that each Nation consumes in the perishable Goods of each Country. But as the Arguments are grounded on a Simile, so they have the Fate of all such Arguments, to be lame, and not run upon all four; according to the saying, Similitudo non currit quatuor pedibus.

For the Stock of a Nation is vastly different from that of a private persons; the one is infinite, the other finite. There is every year a Harvest, a perpetual increase of Cattel, and the Mines can never be exhausted. So that the two thousand pounds in the Chest may be spent, which is a limited Sum; yet the Tin, Lead, Wooll, and those Manufactures that are made of them, can never be consum'd; for no sort of Trade can waste the Stock of a Nation.

But if we consider a Nation as consisting of a Body of People, the inhabitants maybe made richer or poorer; but it is not by consuming the Stock of the Nation, but for want of improving the Stock. It is not by Trading, but for want of Trade. That Nation is accounted rich, when the greatest number of the inhabitants are rich. And they are only made rich by Industry, Arts, and Traffick. By Industry and Art, the Minerals are dug out of the earth, and made useful; the Land made more fertile, by which is produced a greater increase of the Native Stock: And from the profit of this increase of Stock, the People are paid for their Time, Art and Industry, which makes such inhabitants rich. And by Traffick and Commerce the Merchant, Owners of Ships, and Sailers grow rich, by being paid for carrying away the surplus of what is improved more than can be used in the Country, and exchanging it for something that's useful which that Country could not produce; which surplus, if it was not carried away, would by its plenty bring down the Value of the Native Stock, and put a stop to the Labour and Industry of the People, in further improving the Wares of the Country.

It is not material what sort of Foreign Wares the surplus is exchang'd for, whether they are perishable or not, so they do not lessen the Industry of the People; which is easily prevented, by putting such a Duty upon them, as may make them too dear for common use. For the Merchant, and those that are concern'd in the shipping, grow rich, and get as much by importing Wines, Oils, Fruit, and other perishable Goods, as they would do by importing Iron, Copper, Silver, Gold, or other Goods as durable: or perhaps more, because of the bulkiness of the Oils, Wines, &c. which pays a greater Freight than the other Goods. And it is an advantage to the Merchant, and to all Traders in general, that the Goods they deal in are perishable; because there is a continual occasion to make and fetch more as fast as those are spent. And if they were to deal only in Wares that were not perishable, in a short time there would be more imported of such Goods than there was occasion for; and so there would be an end of their Trade, and a stop to the Industry of the People.

So that the question of which Nation thrives most, cannot be determined by observing which imports most Goods in value that are perishable; but by observing which imports most of such sorts of Goods that most increase or lessen the Labour and Industry of the People, and which Nation imports or exports most of such Goods by which the greatest number of the Inhabitants are made rich.

This can never be discern'd by the value of Goods in the Custom-House Books, or by any other Calculation that is propos'd for the taking an account of the Balance of Trade. For tho' a Nation should import and consume less in value of the Foreign Commodities, than are exported of the Native; and the rest, which is the Balance, should be paid in Bullion: yet such a Nation may grow poor, and be undone.

For suppose Antwerp were the Staple for Wooll, (as 'twas formerly, before England had the knowledge of making Cloth) and the English Wooll was carried thither; and in Exchange, the Merchants brought back as much Cloth as was necessary to supply England, and the rest they return'd in Bullion: yet it is plain the Nation would be a great loser by such a Trade, tho' it did not consume so much of their Foreign Cloth in value, as the Flemings did of our Wooll. For by such a Trade, all those that us'd to make the Cloth and Stuff, would grow poor for want of employment, and the Nation would lose the profit of their labour.

And the same Argument might be us'd in exporting of Raw Hides, or any other Commodity that's unwrought. So that it is not from the value of the Goods imported, but from the difference in the nature and quality of the Goods, that makes a Nation richer or poorer.

And the importing of Wines, or any other Commodities that are only for the use of the richer sort of People, which do not hinder the labour and industry of the Nation, areas profitable as the importing, of Bullion. So that the taking an account of the Poverty or Riches of a Nation by such a Balance of Trade from the value of Goods, if such accounts could be taken, would be of no use.

There is but one infallible Symptom to know when Trading Nations thrive and grow rich; that is, when the Inhabitants grow more populous; when they enlarge and new-build their Cities and Towns; and when they increase their Ships and Naval Strength.

I have insisted longer on this Subject than was necessary in this Discourse; and the rather, because the Balance of Trade does so generally perplex all Debates concerning Trade. And that the Notion seems as if it were at first invented by some Merchants, on purpose to mislead Mens Reasons about Trade; because it is commonly us'd for an Argument against any flourishing Trade, That such a Trade is not for the Interest of the Nation.

The Spanish Merchants us'd to cry out against the French. The Turky Company against the East-India Company. And now, all of them against the Dutch. And all their Arguments are drawn from the Balance of Trade. By which Arguments they too often prevail to get Prohibitions, and great Impositions, to lessen such and such Trades, for each Merchant's particular advantage, and too often against the Interest of the Nation.

But to return to the Question; that is, Whether, if the Balance of Trade be against a Nation, the Money will be carried out to pay the Debt, be the Value of it rais'd or not?

And tho' I am of an opinion, there never was any Balance of Trade made up, nor can be by any methods propos'd, as I have yet hear'd of; nor any such uses to be made by it, as is expected, if it could be found out: yet because I cannot think that Gentlemen may on a sudden alter their opinions by any thing that I have wrote, against a Subject so generally believ'd, I will therefore, for Argument's sake, suppose there is a Balance of Trade, and that it is, or may be cast up every year with every Nation; yet it will not follow that the Balance of the Account must be paid in money. For if the Balance be paid by Value, it is no matter by what sort of Goods that Value is paid: For one sort of Wares are as good as another, if the Values be equal. An hundred pounds worth of Lead or Iron, is as good as an hundred pounds worth of Silver or Gold.

The general way of Balancing all Accompts in Foreign Trade, is by Bills of Exchange. For Foreign Exchange is the paying a Sum of Money in one Country, to be repaid the same Sum in the Foreign Coin of another Country; with allowance of Interest for the time of paying it, according to the Agreement; which is call'd with single or double Usance.

In the Infancy of Foreign Trade in England, all Foreign Exchange was made in an Office, set up on purpose to return Bills of Exchange; which Office at first was setled by Act of Parliament, and afterwards the Kings granted Patents for the keeping of it. The last Patent was granted to the Lord Burleigh, then Lord Treasurer, in the Reign of Queen Elizabeth. Those that kept the Office did generally belong to the Mints, and were well acquainted with Bullion and Foreign Coins, but with no other Commodities.

In those days, being the beginning of Foreign Trade, all sorts of Foreign Coins were in all Trading Countries currant. In the United Provinces Foreign Coins were currant till the year 1622, at which time a Placate was set out, forbidding all Foreign Coins to pass any otherwise than as Bullion, by weight; except about half a score sorts of Gold Coins, and as many Silver therein expressed.

In France all Foreign Coins were currant till the year 1614, in the Reign of Lewis XIII.

In those days, all sorts of Money being currant, the Money was often sent over in Specie, from one Country to another to buy Goods, and Balance Accompts. And therefore in the Reign of Harry VIII. the Money in the Kingdom being grown very scarce, there was a great Complaint against the Exchangers, for sending away the Money of the Kingdom; whereupon he ordered a stop upon the Office of Foreign Exchange; and prohibited, for some time, any Foreign Bills to be either accepted or drawn, to prevent the sending away of the Money.

But since Foreign Trade is grown more dispers'd and enlarg'd, almost every Merchant accepts and draws Bills of Exchange. And since no money now passes currant but in that Country where it is coin'd, it is not usual to send over Money in specie to buy Goods, or balance the Accompt: For the Merchants that draw and accept Bills of Exchange being general Traders, and acquainted with the Value of all sorts of Goods; and Money being a Commodity, and reckon'd as Bullion in a Foreign Country, if there be Effects of the same Value to answer the Bill in any sort of Goods, it is the same thing as if Money was sent to answer it. And if the Merchant has no effects in the Countrey where the Bill is to be paid; yet if he has in any Foreign Countrey, to which Bills of Exchange are usually drawn, he may answer his Bill, and pay the Balance of his accompt without Money, by drawing Bills from one place to another where his effects are.

And therefore, when Mr. Lock says, That the Balance of the Foreign accompt must be sent over and paid in Money, he must suppose that the Nation has no other effects in any other Foreign Countrey; but, that they are at the self-same time even every where else, which never was, nor never can be as long as a Nation continues in Trade.

And also that there must be a stop put to Trade, till such an accompt be Balanc'd by the payment of the Money; or else, a Nation that has any effects in Value, might send over Goods to balance the accompt, without sending over their Money.

Besides, some Nations have little or no Bullion in their Countrey; as Denmark, Sueden, and the Northern parts of the World. And yet the Merchants Accompts are as well Paid and Balanc'd, as in any other countrey where there is more plenty of Gold and Silver.

For, as the course of Foreign Trade now is, there is no occasion to send over Money to buy Goods, or Balance the Account; for the Money is paid at the time when the Bill is first drawn: So that there is no occasion to send Money over where the Bill is to be accepted and repaid; and the buying of Goods, or Balancing of the Accompt, is done by the Foreign Money of the Countrey, which is receiv'd from the person that accepts the Bill.

Money is never carried out of any Countrey where it is Coin'd, except it be to those Countries where the Bullion bears a higher price than what the Money is currant at: Or when the Exchange runs so high to any Country, as it will be more profit to the Merchant to melt down the money, and send it over in Bullion, than by Bills of Exchange. And in both these Cases it may often fall out, that the money may be sent over to a Country, and yet no Debt contracted in that Country. And therefore the Balancing the Accompt, can't be the reason of drawing the money out of a Nation.

For tho' Spain were not indebted to any Nation, yet the Gold and Silver would be brought away: For being more plentiful there than in any part of Europe, because of the West-Indies that belong to 'em, is consequently there of a lower Value. And being their chief Staple Commodity, having little other Goods of Value, if they will Trade with other Nations, and have their Commodities, they must give their Bullion in Exchange, tho' their Laws are Capital that prohibit it. And yet every time they Traffick with other Nations, there may be no Debts left on either side.

And the same likewise may be observ'd in the course of Foreign Exchange. For the rise and fall of Foreign Exchange, is from the difference of the Sums that are to be return'd in the Exchange: Just as all sorts of Goods are cheaper or dearer, from their plenty or scarcity; so the Exchange to any place is either higher or lower, according to the greater or lesser quantity of money that is to be return'd by the Exchange. Sometimes an hundred pound may be worth five or ten percent. to be return'd; and a little while after, to the same place, may be worth as much to the contrary. And if it happens when the Exchange is high, that there is as great a conveniency in sending to the same place the Bullion, as there is to get a Bill of Exchange; the Merchant, to save five or ten per cent. will send away the money. And this may fall out, when there is no Debt owing at the place. As to instance:

If a Merchant were to buy Goods at Francfort, or Amsterdam, at the Fair, or East-India Sale; if the Exchange be high, as 'tis generally at those times, he'll send away Bullion thither, rather than Bills, if there be any thing to be got by't, to buy Goods in those places; and yet he might owe nothing there: so that the money is not sent away to Balance the Accompt.

The Inferences from this Discourse of the Balance of Trade, and Foreign Exchange, are:

That a Trading Nation is made Rich by Traffick, and the Industry of the Inhabitants. And that the Native Stock of a Nation can never be wasted.

That no sort of Commodities ought to be totally prohibited. And that the freer the Trade is, the better the Nation will thrive.

That the Poverty and Riches of a Nation, does not depend upon a lesser or greater consumption of Foreign Goods, nor on the difference of the Value of those Goods that are consum'd.

That the Balance of Trade is a Nation that serves rather to puzzle all Debates of Trade, than to discover any particular Advantages that a Nation may get by regulating of Trade.

That the Balance of Trade (if there be one) is not the cause of sending away the Money out of a Nation: But that proceeds from the difference of the Value of Bullion in several Countries, and from the Profit that the Merchant makes by sending it away, more than by the Bills of Exchange.

That there is no Occasion to send away Money or Bullion to pay bills of Exchange, or Balance Accompts.

That all sorts of Goods of the Value of the Bill of Exchange, or the Balance of the Accompt, will answer the Bill, and Balance the Accompt as well as Money.

OF RAISING THE VALUE OF MONEY,

WITH THE CAUSES OF IT,

AND THE EFFECTS.

It has been a Custom in all Ages, and amongst all Nations, to Raise the Value of their Money, and is as Ancient as the Coinage of Money, and not a late Invention, as some are of Opinion.

It was a Custom among the Assyrians, Hebrews and Grecians, as might be made appear, if it were necessary. But, to shew that it was no Modern Invention, will sufficiently appear by the Romans Raising the Value of their Coin. The As, being the Copper Money of the Romans, was at first Coin'd of a pound Weight. And in the first Punick War, in the Dictatorship of Fabius Maximus, it weigh'd but two Ounces, and all the lesser pieces of it were abated in proportion. The As was afterwards reduced to an Ounce, and again by Papirius to half an Ounce. When the Romans began first to Coin Silver Money, the Denarius, which was an Ounce of fine Silver, and about the Value of our Crown, was made current for ten Ases. The Half-Denarius, the Sestertius, and the Sextula, which was Six in an Ounce, were Coin'd to the same proportion. Afterwards the Denarius was Coin'd to Seven in an Ounce; and after that to the Weight of a Drachma, which is Eight in an Ounce: And the lesser parts, as, the Sestertius, Sextula, &c. were abated in proportion.

Their Gold Money was also from time to time Raised: Those Pieces called Solidi Aurei, which were at first Coin'd to Forty Eight Pieces in the pound, were at several times Rais'd. And in the time of Iustinian the Emperor, were coin'd to Seventy two Pieces in the Pound.

The Romans did not only Raise the Value of their Money, by Coining of it Lighter; but they did also Raise it by putting in an Allay, which they did at several times, and by several proportions. And in the time of Livius Drusus, the Allay was so excessive, that the mixture was Eight Ounces Copper, and Four Ounces fine Silver in a Pound Troy. This base Money created a disturbance amongst the People; which was the occasion of that saying in Tully's Offices,

Jactabatur enim illis Temporibus Nummis, Ut nemo sciret quid haberet in Pecunia:

Whereupon Marius Gratidianus, being Triumvir Monetae cudendae, brought in an Ordinance for the Calling in, and Regulating this Money, for which he was in great Esteem amongst the People.

This is sufficient to shew, that the Raising the Value of the Money is no late Invention.

In these Latter Ages all the Kingdoms and States of Europe have from time to time Rais'd the Value of their Money, is very plain. In France, the Ounce of their Standard Silver, which is the French Crown, was at first divided in Sixty Sous, afterwards the Crown was rais'd to Sixty five, and of late to Seventy two Sous: And the New Crown was from time to time made Lighter; that is, the Pound Troy, which contains Twelve Ounces, was at first divided into Twelve Crowns, and afterwards into Thirteen Crowns, and of late into Fourteen Crowns and almost an half. And there are Old Crowns still current in France that have the Stamps upon them, which shew how they have been several times Rais'd.

The Ounce or Dollar of the United Provinces, was at first divided into Thirty six Stivers, afterwards Rais'd to Forty, and since higher, tho' they have another way of Raising their Money, which is, by adding agreater Allay. The Ounce, or Rix-Dollar of the Emperor, which was at first Coin'd at Fifty Crutzers, was Raised to Fifty five, and after that to Sixty. In Spain and Portugal, every Merchant knows that has Traded thither, that the Values, of their Monies have been several times Raised.

In England, from Osbright the Saxon King, till Edward the Third, the Peny was a Peny weight of fine Silver, and the Pound was a Pound Troy Weight of fine Silver. He Rais'd the Value of the Money by putting Eighteen peny Weight of Allay into the Pound Troy. And Mr. Lownds in his Report containing an Essay for the Amendment of the Silver Coins, has given a very exact Account since Edward the Third's Time, taken from the Records of the Mint, how the Money of England has been from time to time Rais'd. By which it appears, that the Silver Peny which in the beginning of his Reign weigh'd a Peny-Weight, there being then but Twenty pence in an Ounce, has been by Degrees, in several Kings Reigns Coin'd lesser and lighter; and the Ounce has been divided into Twenty five pence, Thirty, Thirty seven pence half peny, Forty five pence. And in the beginning of Queen Elizabeth's Reign, the Crown, or Ounce, was divided into Sixty pence: And in the latter end of her Reign into Sixty two pence.

The Standard and course of the Mint has continued to this time without any alteration, except what was made by an Act in the Reign of King Charles II. which gave away the charge of Coinage, being Two shillings in the Pound Troy advantage, for an incouragement to those that brought Bullion into the Mint; which rais'd the price of Bullion to the Nation, instead of raising the Value of the Coin.

The several States and Princes. of Italy have Rais'd their Coins; and if it were necessary, it might be easily prov'd, that there is not one Mint in Europe that has been of any continuance, but has Coin'd their Money lighter then they did at the first beginning of their Coinage.

The way of raising the Value of the Money is not in all Countries alike. In the United Provinces, Flanders, Germany, and the Northern parts of Europe, it has been usually by putting in a greater Allay, and making of it a little courser, and a little lighter.

The Standard of the United States was at first Nine Ounces and an half fine Silver, and Two and an half Allay in the pound Troy: But since, by degrees, their Standard has been brought to Nine Ounces fine, and Three Ounces Allay. And likewise their new Dollars have been Coined lighter; so that the old Dollars that went before at Six and thirty Stivers, were rais'd to Forty. And the same might be observ'd in all the rest of the Mints of Flanders, Germany, and the Northern parts.

In Italy, France, and England, the way of raising their Coin, has been generally by keeping the old Standard for fineness, and only by altering the weight; from time to time Coining their New Money lighter, as they had occasion to raise the Value of their Money.

In Portugal and Spain, the usual method of raising their Money has not been by altering their Standard either in fineness or weight; but by giving a Rise to their Money, by a Computation made from the Value of the Copper Money; that is, a Riall of Eight, which in Spain was formerly of the Value of Three hundred and seventy Malvedies, was raised to pass currant for Four hundred Malvedies, which is their Copper Money, and so higher from time to time.

And the same is to be observ'd in Portugal: They raise the Value of their Money by their Reas, which is their Copper Money. And the Ducat, or Crusado, that us'd to pass for Four hundred Reas, has been rais'd to Four hundred and fifty, and higher.

The usual Proportion of Value that Princes and States give to their Silver and Gold Money when they Raise the Value of them, is generally betwixt Ten and Fifteen per cent. above the Market-price of Silver and Gold. The French Crown was Raised from Sixty Sous, to Sixty five, which is about Ten percent. And about three or four Years since, the Crown was Raised to Seventy two Sous, which is near Fifteen per cent. The Rix-Dollar, Coin'd at Fifty Stivers, was Raised to Fifty five Stivers, and since to Sixty, which is about Ten per cent.

The Kings of England have Rais'd their Money from Twenty, to Twenty five, Thirty, Thirty seven, &c. which is after the same proportion as the Emperor, the French King, and other Princes and States have done.

The Dutch raise the Value of their Money by adding a greater Allay (as has been observ'd) which is less taken notice of, and so does not disturb the minds of those persons who think the value of Money is solely from the quantity of fine Silver in each piece.

The Reason why Princes and States do observe to give no greater Proportion of Value to their Money when they new raise it, than betwixt Ten and Fifteen per cent. above the currant price of Bullion, is, to prevent counterfeiting.

For tho' there are Laws in all Countries, with severe Penalties, to prohibit the counterfeiting of Money, yet none are kept and observed, where there is great Profit to begot by breaking of them. And no persons will counterfeit the Stamp, and make the

Money the same both in weight and fineness, for only Ten or Fifteen per cent. Profit. For they must Coin a great quantity, to make their Profit considerable; if they make the Money of the same weight and fineness, it will not be One hundred and forty pound clear Profit in Coining of a Thousand pound at Fifteen per cent. because of the charge of Coinage. And none but the rich man can vent a great quantity, and he'll not hazard the loss of his Life and Estate for such small Gain. The poor man cannot attempt it, because he can neither get Bullion to Coin, nor vent a quantity after 'tis Coin'd. And why should any man venture his Life for such small Profit, when every Merchant and Tradesman gets more without any such hazard?

Therefore those that coin false Money, counterfeit the Metal as well as the Stamp, to make it profitable. But then it is much easier discovered, and they are often punish'd with death: For they must counterfeit the weight, colour, and size of the Piece, as well as the Stamp; which is much more difficult than only to counterfeit the Stamp.

So that the Princes and States may as safely coin their Money Ten or Fifteen per cent. above the price of Bullion, without danger of counterfeiting, as if they should coin it exactly to the Market-price.

The Reason why the Princes and States, when they have rais'd the Value of their Money, have not coin'd it nearer to the price of Bullion, than about the difference of Ten per cent. is to avoid the too often raising the Value of their Coin; which, when ever it is done, is apt to create some little murmur and discontent amongst the People. And if they should coin it near the Value, they would be forced to raise their Money as oft as Silver rises in its price above the Value of the Coin, which would be every Five or Ten Year; whereas by raising of it betwixt Ten of Fifteen per cent. they have not usually rais'd it but once in Fifty or Threescore Years.

As to instance from Edward the Third's time to Queen Elizabeth, which was betwixt Two hundred and fifty, and Three hundred Years from the first raising of the Money, from Twenty pence in an Ounce of Silver to Threescore pence, is betwixt Ten or Twelve per cent. for every Fifty Years. And the like might be observ'd, if it were necessary, in all the Mints of Europe.

In the Reign of Edward VI. when there was so great an Allay put into the Money as rais'd it to Forty or Fifty per cent. profit above the price of Silver, there were Barrels of counterfeit Money seiz'd at the Custom-house, that were sent from Foreign parts. The knowledge of that created so great a jealousy and disturbance in the minds of the People, that scarce any Money would pass, for fear of receiving that which was counterfeit.

For the knowledge of the goodness of Silver, is a Mystery that few are acquainted with; and when there is so great an Allay put into the Money, those that counterfeit may make the Metal as good, if not better than the true Money, because there's profit sufficient by only counterfeiting the Stamp. And that may be so well imitated, as not one in a thousand may discover the difference betwixt the true and the false Stamp. And tho' the Metal may be as good or better than the true Money, yet it being counterfeited, it's none of the Government's Money. And wanting their Authority, by which it is made currant, no man is oblig'd to take it; and therefore every body refuses the Money in general, for fear the loss should fall upon him that last takes it; so that the Money becomes useless, having lost the currancy and quality of Money, and all the murmur and disorder ensues that usually attends a Nation that want Money to drive their Trade and Commerce.

Other Instances might be given, but this, with the common usage of not exceeding Ten or Fifteen per cent. when the Money is rais'd, may be sufficient to answer Mr. Lock's Objection,

That the Governments cannot raise their Money as high as they please; nor make themselves as Rich as they please.

The great Objection that Mr. Lock makes against the raising the Value of Money, is, That if the Government have a Power to give a Value of Ten per cent. to their Money, why not Twenty, Fifty, or as high as they please? And then it would be in the Government's Power at any time to make themselves as rich as they please.

Such a Power, at this time, were to be wish'd for, when the Nation is engag'd in so chargeable a War: But that's the misfortune that attends us, that such a Power can be only wish'd for.

For tho' Princes and States have a Power to give a Value to their Money, yet that Power is limited. And when ever they have attempted to exceed those Limits, which upon an extraordinary emergency they have sometimes done, they have fallen under greater mischiefs, by reason the Money has been always counterfeited, than the advantages they propos'd to themselves amounted to by doing of it; and have always been forc'd to call in such Money, and reduce the Value within its usual limits and bounds.

There are two Causes why Princes and States raise the Value of their money; the one is Ordinary, and the other Extraordinary.

The Ordinary and Common Cause of Raising the Value of the Coin, is the Rise of Bullion.

Gold and Silver are Commodities for other Uses, besides the making of money; as for making of Plate, Lace, Gilding, &c. And besides, it's scarcer in some Countries, and more plenty in others: And the Value of all things arising from their Occasions; and Plenty and Scarcity making things cheap and dear; when ever the Goldsmiths, and the Makers of Plate, Lace, &c. and the Merchants to export it to the Indies, or those Countries where 'tis more scarce, will give more for Bullion to supply such occasions, than the Mints can afford to do, according to the Value the money is at, the Princes and States have been forced from time to time to raise the Value of their Coin to prevent it from being melted down, and carried away.

The knowledge when Bullion is risen above the Value of the money, is discover'd by the Mints: For the Mints are the common Shops and Market place for the Merchants to carry in their Bullion. And when ever they forbear the bringing of it thither, it is certain it will yield them a better price in another place: For Bullion never continues long in a place unalter'd, because it yields no profit while it continues so. But if it be carried to the Mint to be Coin'd, it becomes useful for Trade and Commerce, and saves the charge of borrowing money, or else may be put out to Interest. And if it be wrought into Plate, Lace, &c. it pays for the fashion and workmanship. And if it be transported to the Indies, or some Country where it's dearer, it produces profit by the exchange of those Goods that are bought with it.

When ever any of the Princes and States in Europe Raise the Value of their Coin, the rest generally follow. It were too long to give particular Instances; but if it be examin'd by the Records of the Mints of the Kings of France, with those of the Mints of the Kings of England, it will appear, that they have Rais'd their Money from time to time, as the Kings of England have done, or rather higher. For that, since the time of St. Lewis, who was co-temporary with Edward the IIId. the Sols and Crowns contained then near six times more of fine Silver, than the Sols and French Crowns do that are lately Coin'd; which is a greater proportion than the Money has Risen in England since Edward the Third's Time, being not quite four times lighter: The reason is, it's almost a hundred years since the English have Raised the Value of their Silver Coin; and in the same time the French have Rais'd theirs twice; which would have made the English Money much of the same Rise, with giving of allowance to the custom of the English, who have always undervalued their Silver Money, and overvalued their Gold, in respect to their Neighbour Nations; and have since twice Rais'd the value of their Gold; to wit, in King Iames the First's time, who Coin'd a twenty-Shilling-piece of Gold lighter by Two shillings, than that which he Coin'd in the beginning of his Reign; which rais'd the value of his first Jacobus's to Two and Twenty Shillings. And in King Charles the Second's time, who Coin'd the Guinea Two shillings lighter than the Broad-Piece: So that when the Guinea was currant at Twenty shillings, the Broad-Piece went for Two and Twenty.

There seems to be an absolute necessity for the Princes and States of Europe to Raise the value of their Money much about the same time, or else they cannot preserve it in their Countries, notwithstanding any severe Laws to prohibit the Melting and Exporting of it. For there being a constant Commerce and Traffick betwixt all the Countries of Europe; If one Prince sets a much higher value on his Money than another, the Merchants, whose business it is to observe where they can get most profit, will melt down the Coin of one Countrey, and carry it to the Mint of another Countrey, where the Money is Rais'd, and will yield the greatest price.

This will appear plain by an Instance herein England: For the Kings of England having not Rais'd their Silver Money since the Reign of Queen Elizabeth, which is about a hundred years ago; and the rest of the Princes and States of Europe having since that time twice rais'd their several Coins, to wit, in the Reign of King James the First, and about Four or Five years since: That although there has been since that time Coin'd in England (with allowance of what was Coin'd in Queen Elizabeth's Reign) the Sum of 19429061 l. 19 s. 6 d. as appears by the Records of the Mint; yet by the Computation that Mr. Lownds makes, there is not above Five Millions Six hundred thousand pounds remaining; which, in my opinion, is more than will be found to be, upon the new Coinage of the Money, by the calculation he makes from the Worn and Clipp'd Money. So that there has been near Fourteen Millions melted down and carried away within this space of time. And had it not been for some accidental causes that brought Bullion to the Mint since the Foreign Princes have rais'd the value of their Coins, there had been very little Silver Money Coin'd, and much less to be found now in England.

For in King Charles the First's time, by the Civil Wars of England, the Plate was brought to the Mints to be Coin'd; which was the cause of the great sum of Silver Money Coin'd in his Reign.

The Calling in the Parliament-Money in King Charles the Second's time, and new Coining of it: The Two or Three hundred thousand pounds that were yearly sent into England from France, upon some particular occasions during his Reign, with the Money that Dunkirk was sold for: And the Act of Parliament for giving away the charge of Coinage, to incourage the Merchants to bring Bullion to the Mint, being almost Three and an Half per cent. were the occasion of the Silver money Coin'd in his Reign. And if the two Sums Coined in these two Kings Reigns, which make about Twelve Millions, with the Money that was Coin'd in Queen Elizabeth's Reign, and a Million that was Coin'd in the Reign of King James the First, before the Foreign Princes Rais'd the value of their Coins, be put together, they will make near eighteen Millions: So that were it not for these accidental Causes, there had not been Coin'd in the Mint of England Two Millions of Silver Money since the Foreign Princes Rais'd the Value of their Coins. And had it not been for the wearing of some of the old

Money lighter by often telling it over; and Clipping of the rest, by which they were made unprofitable to melt down, by this time, in all probability, there had scarce been a Silver piece of Money to be seen in England.

And that the Raising the Coin in Foreign parts, and the not Raising the Silver Coin in England, was the cause of melting it down, and Transporting it, will plainly appear from the plenty of the Gold here compared with the Silver. For, since the Forty third of Queen Elizabeth, being the last time that the Silver Money was rais'd here in England, the Gold has been twice greatly rais'd; by which means, there is here double, if not treble the quantity of Gold for Silver; whereas in all other Kingdoms and States in Europe, there is ten times more Silver Money than Gold.

For in the Forty third Year of Queen Elizabeth (according to Mr. Lownds's account from the Records of the Mint, which all men agree is very exact) a pound weight Troy of Gold of the Standard of Twenty two Carats fine, and Two Carats Allay, was Coin'd into Thirty three Soveraigns and an half, at Twenty shillings a piece, making Thirty three pounds ten shillings.

In the Reign of King James I. the Gold was rais'd, and the same pound weight and standard of Gold was coin'd into as many Units, Double-Corowns, and other pieces of Gold, as made up Forty pound eighteen shillings and four pence.

And in King Charles the Second's time, the Gold was again rais'd, and the same standard and weight was coin'd into Forty four Guineas and an half, at Twenty shillings apiece. So that from Thirty three pound ten shillings in Queen Elizabeth's time, to Forty four pound ten shillings in King Charles's Reign, the Gold was rais'd near Three and thirty per cent. since the Silver money has been rais'd; which is the reason of the great plenty of Gold, and scarcity of Silver. What was the reason that these two Princes rais'd their Gold, and not their Silver, is not to be imagin'd; unless it was from some powerful Argument offer'd by the Guiney Company, whose Interest it is to have Gold rais'd; which does not appear.

And that this raising the Gold is the cause that it is more plentiful here in England than Silver, will appear yet more plain, if the Records of the Mint be examin'd since King Charles the Second's Restauration: For since that time there has been coin'd in the Mint of England 7263836 l. 1 s. 5 d. and in Silver but 4319585 l. 9 s. 5 d. which does not want much of double the quantity of Gold Money that has been coin'd more than Silver.

And when the Guineas had an extraordinary Rise here in England, as to be currant at Eight and twenty and Thirty shillings apiece, there was above Seven hundred and twenty thousand pounds in Gold coin'd in little more than Nine months time; which was more than was coin'd in six or eight Years before; which shews plainly, that the raising the Value of the Gold money here in England, is the cause that so much is imported and coin'd here. And on the contrary, the not raising of the Silver money in proportion, as the Foreign Mints have done, is the cause of its being constantly melted down, and carried away, notwithstanding the many Laws to prohibit it.

For there are severe Laws in all Kingdoms and States, that prohibit the counterfeiting, clipping, melting, and exporting the money. In all Countries 'tis death to counterfeit and clip the money. In France, England, and several other Countries, it is a high Crime to melt it down, and forfeiture of the money to export it; and in Spain, 'tis death to transport it. And yet, when ever it has been profitable, it has been always melted down, and carried away. So that by experience Princes and States have found, that there is no other way to preserve it in the Country, but by raising the Value of their money so much above the price of Bullion, that the Merchant may get more by carrying away the Bullion, than the Money.

The cause of raising the Money here in Europe will always continue, as long as the Europeans continue in Traffick and Commerce; for Trade makes a People rich, and Gold and Silver are Badges of Riches; and therefore as the People grow rich, the price of Gold and Silver will rise, because the occasions for Gold and Silver will still increase.

Especially as long as the Trade continues to the Mogul's Country in the East-Indies: For the Princes and great People there believe; that the possession of Gold and Silver is not only an Honour to them while they are alive, but that they shall have a Respect in the next World, according to the quantity of Gold and Silver they die possess'd of: And therefore what-ever Gold and Silver they get more than is absolutely necessary for Commerce and Traffick, they from time to time melt into a Mass, or Tank, which is buried with them; so that great part of what's dug out of the West, is buried in the East.

And altho' there have been great quantities of Gold and Silver brought into Europe since the Discovery of the West-Indies, yet the price of them has always risen; and will always continue so, as long as the People grow rich by Trade; which will make the occasions for them greater than the quantity, which is the Rule by which all things are made dear.

This continual Rise of Gold and Silver will be no prejudice to the Princes and States, if they do but observe to raise and keep up their money above the price of Silver and Gold; for there will be the same quantity of Silver and Gold in the Country, tho' the money be lighter. And the difference will be only, that there will be more in every man's House, and less in his Pocket. And the money will have the same Value, tho' the impressions be less, because it has its Value from the Authority of the Government: Just as if the Ingraver should cut the impression of the Great Seal less, it would not alter the

Authority of the Seal.

This may be sufficient to prove, That the Ordinary Cause of Raising the Value of the Money, is from the Rise of Bullion; which will always continue in Europe, as long as the Inhabitants grow rich by Trade.

The Extraordinary Cause of raising the Value of money, has been the Extraordinary Occasion for it. When Princes and States have been engag'd in great Wars, and wanting money, they have sometimes rais'd the Value of it to increase it, and make it last longer; In such Cases they have not observ'd the usual Bounds and Limits of raising the Value of money Ten or Fifteen per cent. above the Market price of Bullion; but have greatly exceeded it to Thirty, Forty, Fifty percent. and more. But then, in all such Cases, as soon as those extraordinary occasions were over, they have call'd in such money as has been so greatly rais'd, and reduc'd the Value of it to its usual Bounds.

In the first Punick War, the Romans wanting money, rais'd the Value of the As, which was their Brass Coin, to six times more in Value than it was coin'd at; it weighing at first twelve Ounces, and afterwards but two. And again wanting money, Hannibal pressing hard upon the City, they increased their money, by coining the As to an Ounce. And the third time, Papirius raised the money to double its Value, by coining it at half an Ounce. They also rais'd their Denarius, which was their Silver money, in proportion. By which they carried on the War against the Carthagenians, and suppli'd themselves under great Necessities, and want of money. Livius Drusus also greatly rais'd the Value of the Silver money, by putting in a great Allay: But these excessive Rises were afterwards regulated and reduc'd by Marius Gratidianus.

In the Wars betwixt England and France, Harry the Fifth having conquer'd great part of France, Charles the Seventh rais'd the Value of the French money in six Years time, from

Eight Livres, Nine Sols, the Mark, by degrees to Three hundred and sixty Livres, the Mark: which was rais'd, in that time, above Forty times the Value. And as those that write of the Mints of France observe,'twas the chief means by which he expell'd the English out of France. But as soon as ever the War was over, he reduc'd the money to Seven Livres Ten Sols; which was within the usual Limits of raising the money. At the same time Harry the Fifth raised the money of England from Twenty five shillings in a Pound weight, to Thirty. And Harry the Sixth, his Son, the next Year rais'd it to Thirty seven and six-pence: so that it was rais'd a third part more in Value in two Years time, than it had been ever since the Twenty seventh of Edward the Third. Andin the Fourth Year of Harry the Sixth, after Charles the Seventh had reduc'd his money, he lower'd the English money again to 30 s.

When Harry the Eighth alter'd the Standard of England, and extraordinarily rais'd the Value of the money by putting in a great Allay; which alteration at first was by putting in but two Ounces Allay, to ten Ounces of fine Silver; afterwards six Ounces, and at last eight Ounces Allay, to four Ounces of fine Silver. By which, in three Years time, he rais'd the Value of the money above three times higher than it was before; but it was when he had spent his money in the War of Bullen. And the Nation was never at peace and quiet in their Commerce and Traffick, till the Value of the money was reduc'd within its Bounds; which was begun by Edward the Sixth, and finish'd by Q. Elizabeth.

These are the Extraordinary Causes of raising the Value of money, to supply Extraordinary Necessities; which have no sooner been over, but the Value of the money has been reduc'd within its usual Limits: For if the Rise had been continued, the Mischiefs would have been greater than the Advantages they receiv'd, by raising it so high. And there can be no Rule or

Measure taken of the Value that the money may be rais'd to from such Presidents, but only from the ill effects in continuing it.

The Effects of Raising the Value of the Money, are:

That it increases the species of the Money, and preserves it in the Countrey where 'tis Coin'd. If the English Crown were Rais'd to Six shillings, or Coin'd in such a proportion lighter, there will be a Sixth part more Money in England than if it be Coin'd to the old Standard. And, if the Money be Rais'd above the price of Bullion, it will not be the Interest of Goldsmiths and Merchants to melt it down. From both which Effects a Nation receives great Advantage.

Mr. Lock is of a contrary opinion, and thinks that the Raising of the Money will produce Two great Mischiefs, viz.

> That the Raising the Value of the Money will Raise the Value of all Commodities.

> That the Landlords and Creditors will lose just so much in their Rents, Bonds, Debts, and Contracts, as the Money is Rais'd.

These are the Two great Objections that are commonly us'd in all Debates about Raising the Value of the Money; and are grounded upon this supposition, That the Value of the Money is solely from the quantity of Silver in each piece; and that 'tis the quantity of Silver that in Buying and Selling, Men give, take, and contract for: So that if there be less Silver in the Money, men will have less Goods for it; and just so much as the Money is Rais'd in Value, the Goods will Rise: And the same Consequence will be if the Landlords did let their Land according to the quantity of Silver in the Money; they will lose just so much Rent if the Money be Rais'd, as it has less Silver in it: And so will the Creditors in their Bonds, Debts, and Contracts.

But if it appear by what has been said on this Subject, and that Mr. Lock is mistaken in his supposition, That the Money has its Value from the Authority of that Government where it is Coin'd, by which it is made Current and Lawful Money: And that 'tis the Current and Lawful Money of England that men contract and sell their Goods for, and in their Bonds and Leases Covenant to pay, Then there will be no such ill effects from Raising of the Old Money, and Coining the New Lighter.

And if it be true, That the Plenty or Scarcity of all Commodities, in respect to their occasion, makes them Cheaper or Dearer; And that the Plenty of one Commodity do's not make another Commodity dearer or cheaper that is not for the same use; then the Plenty of Gold and Silver, or a greater or lesser quantity of it in the money, will no more alter the price of Goods, than the Plenty of Lead or Iron can alter the price of Butter or Cheese, which are not to supply the same Occasions. And Mr. Lock in Page 52 seems to be of this opinion, and answers himself, tho' he concludes quite otherwise.

He says, Corn it is evident do's not rise or fall by the difference of more or less plenty of Money; but, by the plenty and scarcity that God gives. For our Money in appearance remaining the same, the price of Corn is double one year, to what it was the precedent: But from thence infers, we must certainly make account, that if the Money be made a fifth Lighter, it will buy one fifth less Corn Communibus Annis. I must confess I cannot understand this consequence, when in the beginning he says, Corn do's not rise and fall from the difference of the Money.

For, if the Lightness or Heaviness of the Money had any influence over the price of Commodities, then all sorts of Commodities ought to be cheap when the Money is Heavy, and dear when the Money is Light: And the price of things could never alter, but when the Money alters; for the cause being the same, the Effects ought to be the same.

Whereas it is plain some Goods never alter their price: As the Beer and Ale that's sold: The Brewer runs the Risque of the dearness of the Coals, Hops, and Mault. When those Goods are dear, he gains less by Brewing; but always sells his Beer and Ale at one price, let the Money be what it will: Other Goods, such as all sorts of Grain, Coals, and other Commodities alter their price almost every Month: And the Coals are sometimes but half the value to what they were the Month before. So that if these different Alterations in prices arose from the value of the Money, it will follow that both the good and bad Money makes things dear as well as cheap; and the same cause at the same time to have two contrary effects, which cannot be.

But to conclude with answering this Objection, If the Arguments that have been already us'd to shew that Money has not its Value from the quantity of Silver in each piece, do not satisfy; I would advise such Gentlemen always to receive their Money by Weight, and try if they can introduce such a custom: For, they can never have their Money equal by Tale: For, if any man receives and Hundred pounds, and divides it into Five twenties, there will be the difference (unless it be all new Money) of five or ten shillings in the Weight of some of the twenty pounds, tho' by the Tale they are even.

As to the Objection that Mr. Lock makes from a simile when he says, That Money is the Measure of Commerce and Traffick; so that if the Money be made lighter, 'twould be the same thing as if the Government should cut their Yard shorter. The Cloth that is measur'd by such a Yard would be so much less; and so will the quantity of the Goods be that are bought with the Money that's made lighter. It is grounded upon the same supposition, and would be true, if Money were the measure of Commerce by the quantity of Silver in each piece. But if it be the Measure of Commerce from the Authority of the Government; if the Authority be the same, the Measure will no more be alter'd by making the Money lighter, than if the Yard were split in two, so that the length be not alter'd, it will then make two Yards, and measure as much Cloth as if it had not been split, tho' there be but half the quantity of Wood in each Yard.

As to the other Objection of the Landlords and Creditors, That if the Money should be made lighter, they'l lose so much in their Rents, Debts, and Contracts. The Answer is; That the Money having its Value from the Authority of the Government, is always of the same Goodness and Value. And that the Money, if it were made Lighter, would be as good to all purposes, as Money, as it was in the Reign of Harry the Sixth, when it had double the weight of Silver in it, which would be no advantage but to those that melt it: And therefore they cannot lose in their Rents, Debts, &c. if the Money be always of the same Value.

And if they are not satisfied with the Arguments that have been us'd to prove that Money has its Value from the Authority of the Government; That such persons may not be losers in their imagination, if the Parliament should think fit to alter the Standard, and raise the Crown to Six shillings, they shall have my Vote for a Proviso in the Act, That all such persons that have let their Land, or lent Money upon Mortgage, Bonds, or Contracts, within these last one or two and twenty years, (which is as long as Leases are Let, and longer then Mortgages or Bonds generally continue) shall have the same weight of Money paid them out of the Exchequer, as the Money Weigh'd when they Let such Land, or Lent it upon Bonds, Mortgages, or Contracts. And because such Gentlemen, perhaps, may not keep an account of what their money weigh'd then, let the accompt be taken from the Teller's Book in the Exchequer, it being their custom to weigh every Hundred pounds after 'twas told, and enter the weight in their Books, and put a Ticket of the weight to the Bag, to save 'em the trouble of telling the money twice. By this Proposal such Gentlemen will have no reason to complain; for, according to their own opinion, if they have the same weight of Silver they can't be losers. And yet, I believe the Government would be a gainer by the Proposition, though the money were Coin'd a Sixth part lighter than according to the present Standard.

For if those Books were examin'd, perhaps it will be found, that an Hundred Pound has not weigh'd, one Bag with another, Seven and twenty Pound, for these last One or two and twenty Years; whereas it ought to weigh. according to the Standard, Thirty two Pound three Ounces. By such a Proviso these Gentlemen being sav'd, they may thereupon consent to the raising of the money, to prevent those great Inconveniences which, in my opinion, will certainly follow, if the money be not rais'd.

There is another Objection which some Gentlemen use against Raising the Value of the Money, That it will be a Discredit to the Nation, to make their Money lighter. And in their Arguments contend much for the Honour of the Standard of England, and think it is their Duty to defend it: And that His Majesty's Money ought to be of as great Weight and Value as His Predecessors; being of the opinion, That the Money has its sole Value from the quantity of Silver in it.

By this Argument, in my opinion, they seem to be but young Courtiers, and make an ill sort of Compliment to His Majesty, by giving a greater Value and Respect to the Metal, than to the Effigies of the King, when they won't allow that the Stamp and Effigies upon the Coin, gives a Value to the money, and that the King's Authority makes it currant; when all the Coins of his Predecessors were no otherwise made the current money of England, but by their Proclamation.

These are the chief Objections against Raising the Value of

the Money, which, I hope, I have fully answer'd, and shewn, That they are only imaginary Mischiefs. But if the Money be not Rais'd, the Mischiefs will be real, and Consequences very fatal to the Nation.

For, if the money be new-coin'd according to the old Standard, it will be certainly melted down, and carried away as fast as 'tis Coin'd, notwithstanding all the Laws that can be made to prevent it, and the Nation be left without money: The Consequence whereof will be; That Trade will beat a stand; The prices of all Commodities will fall; And a general Poverty and Clamour over the whole Nation ensue.

For Money is the measure of Commerce; And for a Nation to be without money, is the same thing as if it were without measures, and had neither Yards, Scales, nor Bushels in the Country; without some of which, no Bargain can be made.

In those Countries where the Inhabitants do not live upon Trade, but a Country-life, every man having always Provisions sufficient to sustain life, they may shift without money, and barter one Commodity for another. But in England, where the great Body of the People depend upon Trade, and that by selling of such Goods, the greatest part of which the People are under no great necessity of having, but may shift without; and have no way of feeding themselves but by the profit of such Bargains, they cannot live without money; and if there were no money, would starve, because no persons will barter for those Goods that they have no absolute occasion for, if they want money.

Besides, the want of money in a Nation, will bring down the price of all Commodities; for according to the Consumption of all Goods, and the occasion there is for 'em, the price will rise. When money is wanting, men consume less: They are better Husbands, and make every thing last longer; which lessens the consumption of the Native Commodities, and makes the price of them to fall; and if the price of the Native Commodities fall, the Rents of the Land will sink: For the Tenants cannot pay the same Rent, when the Corn and Wooll, and other Commodities, which are the Product of the land, fall to half the Value.

To conclude; There is nothing so much the Interest of the Nation, as at this time to raise their Money. It will increase the speties of the Coin, and save the Nation near a Million of Money, now they are engag'd in a chargeable War. And if there were no other Reason but this, which has been the cause that several Princes and States have rais'd their Money, and have found great Success by't, it were an Argument sufficient.

For if all the money should be new-coin'd to the old Standard, it would not produce much above half the quantity of the money before it was new-coin'd And there might be several Instances given beside that of the Romans and French, where Princes and States have Rais'd their money in time of War, on purpose to increase the quantity of it: But not on President, where by new-coining of it in the time of War, the quantity has been made less.

Besides, There is a greater Reason for Raising the money, while the War continues in Foreign Part because, during the continuance of the Army in Flanders, the Exchange to those places will he high because of the constant occasion to remit money to those Parts to pay the Army. But if the money be Rais'd above the price of Bullion, the Dutch or Flemish Merchants that pay the Bills of Exchange in Flanders with their money, with which the Army is paid, will send for their Effects in Bullion, or the Native Commodities of England, because it will be more profitable to them if the money be Rais'd; but if it be not Rais'd, it will be more profitable to melt down the money, and send it away, than Bills of Exchange. By which, in a short time, there will be no money left in the Nation.

For, the Merchant is paid for the remitting the money, at the first making of the Bargain; and none ever expected to make an advantage by melting down the money of the Country, and sending it away. For, if so, the Merchant need not pay for the Bill of Exchange. But he proposes to have his Return made of his Bill, by the Goods and Effects of the Country from whence the Bill was sent, and that will be much more for the advantage of the Nation; for the Stock of the Nation is perpetual. There is a new Crop of Corn and Wooll every Year, and the Mines are never to be exhausted. And the paying of the Foreign Bills with the Native Stock of the Country, which is the usual way that all Foreign Bills are paid, can never prejudice a Nation.

Besides, If it were not in a time of War, the Silver money ought to be Rais'd, because the Foreign Princes have Rais'd their money twice, since the Silver money has been Rais'd in England. And 'tis the constant usage of all the Foreign Princes and States in Europe, to set a pretty equal Valuation upon their money above the price of Bullion, and to Raise their money much about the same time; or else the money of the Country where 'tis not Rais'd, would be melted down by the Merchants, and carried to the Mints of those Countries where it is Rais'd, and the Bullion yields a greater profit; and so, in a short time, there would be no money left in that Country. The truth of which has been sufficiently shewn from the great quantity of Silver money, being above Fifteen Millions, that has been melted down since the Silver money was Rais'd in England; and there will be the same Consequence, if the money be now coin'd to the old Standard, because the money is of more Value when 'tis melted into Bullion, than in Coin.

Some are of opinion, that the way to keep the Silver Money in the Nation, is to sink the price of the Gold; And would have Guineas brought to Two and twenty, believing that the Silver Money will be bought up by the Gold, and exported. By this way of arguing, they must agree that Silver is of a greater Value in another Country; or else, there would be no advantage got by exporting it. And if the Gold be set at Two and Twenty, or Five and twenty, it won't preserve the Silver; because every Merchant and Trader may take the Silver Money by the Sale of his Goods, and need not buy it with the Gold. And if Guineas be sunk to Two and twenty, it will be a severe Loss to those People that have taken them at higher Rates; And a damage to the Nation, by lessning the quantity of the Coin; and by low'ring the price of them, may cause them to be exported: So that there will be neither Gold nor Silver left in the Nation.

To conclude this Discourse: If nothing in it self has a certain Price or Value; If Gold and Silver are Commodities of uncertain Values. If Money has its Value from the Authority of the Government, which makes it currant, and fixes the price of each piece of Metal; Then the Money will be of as good Value, to all intents and purposes. when it is coin'd lighter. For, the Authority being the same, the Value will be the same. It will buy as much Goods: The Landlord will have as much Rent; And the Nation will save a Million of Money at a time when they haves o great occasion for it. Besides the preventing those fatal Consequences that follow the Coining the Money too weighty; As, The Loss of the Money; Decay of Trade; The Fall of Rents; And a general Poverty and Clamour all over the Nation.

FINIS.

ALSO AVAILABLE FROM NEWTON PAGE

ALSO AVAILABLE FROM NEWTON PAGE

The Mississippi Bubble

A Memoir of John Law

Adolphe Thiers

ISBN-13: 978-1934619056

An established classic and authoritative historical analysis of the spectacular rise and fall of the most enigmatic genius in financial and economic history. It provides a compelling biographical narrative of John Law's life, a considered examination of his Mississippi Scheme, and enlightening accounts of both the Darien Expedition and South Sea Bubble.

ALSO AVAILABLE FROM NEWTON PAGE

Letters to John Law

A Letter to Mr. Law
The Case of Mr. Law Truly Stated
A Second Letter to Mr. Law

Selected and introduced by

Gavin John Adams

ISBN-13: 978-1-934619087

This collection of three uncompromising early eighteenth-century propagandist pamphlets documents the wildly contrasting reactions to Law's surprise return to Britain. Crafted by the most prominent journalists, commentators and political agitators of the day, each provides an invaluable contemporaneous social, political and historical record of the most remarkable story in financial history.

Made in United States
Orlando, FL
04 November 2026

90204181R00143